Teenage Religion and Values

Leslie J Francis

D J James Professor of Pastoral Theology, Trinity College, Carmarthen
and University of Wales, Lampeter

William K Kay

Senior Research Fellow, Centre for Theology and Education,
Trinity College, Carmarthen

Gracewing.

Pellegrini

858 HAY ST, PERTH.
TEL : 321 6655 FAX : 321 1937

First published in 1995

Gracewing
Fowler Wright Books
2 Southern Ave, Leominster
Herefordshire HR6 0QF

Gracewing books are distributed

In New Zealand by
Catholic Supplies Ltd
80 Adelaide Road
Wellington
New Zealand

In Australia by
Charles Paine Pty Ltd
8 Ferris Street
North Parramatta
NSW 2151 Australia

In USA by
Morehouse Publishing
PO Box 1321
Harrisburg
PA 17105 USA

In Canada by
Meakin and Associates
Unit 17, 81 Aurega Drive
Nepean, Ontario
KZE 7Y5, Canada

Cover illustration by Gill Onions

Typesetting by Reesprint, Radley, Oxfordshire, OX14 3AJ

Printed at Redwood Books, Trowbridge, Wiltshire.

ISBN 0 85244 282 3

Teenage Religion and Values

Contents

Preface

This book is part of a major ongoing initiative within the Centre for Theology and Education at Trinity College, Carmarthen, designed to explore the place of religion and values in the lives of young people today. Over the next year or two we aim to extend this database to 25,000 teenagers and to analyse the data from a number of perspectives. This is an unique and valuable resource both for the churches and for secular groups concerned with the development of personal, social and moral values among young people.

Already a consortium of Christians concerned with the churches' work among young people has responded to an invitation issued by the Centre for Theology and Education at Trinity College and Crusaders to reflect on the practical implications of the findings presented in this book. This invitation has led to the publication of a major new text on Christian youth work, *Fast Moving Currents* (Lynx, 1995).

The organisation of such a significant database is both time-consuming and expensive. We are grateful to all those who helped in many ways. At the top of our list of acknowledgements come the headteachers, staff and pupils who responded so positively to the invitation to provide data. Without their time, cooperation and openness there would have been no information on which to base this study. Second, we acknowledge the significant role of the Principal and Governors of Trinity College, Carmarthen, in actively seeking to promote such research initiatives through the newly established Centre for Theology and Education. Third, we are indebted to several trusts and organisations which have sponsored specific parts of the survey, including the Crusader organisation, the Rank Foundation, the Hockerill Educational Foundation, the All Saints' Educational Trust and the Friends First Day Schools Fund. Finally we record our gratitude to Susan

Jones who supervised the data management and Anne Rees and Diane Drayson who helped shape the manuscript.

Leslie J Francis
William K Kay

Trinity College Carmarthen
August 1994

1 Introduction

Because of rapid social and economic change in the western world, the experience of adolescence today is not the same as it was a generation ago. Some things stay the same, yet many change. Even physical development has been occurring very slightly earlier (Wellings *et al*, 1994). But changes and fluctuations in the job market, sexual morality, the incidence of hard and soft drugs, long-term parental unemployment, the numbers of single parent families and educational provision make an impact on teenage life and values.

The teenager stands between the changing world of childhood and the changing world of adulthood. He or she may be reflected in *Grange Hill*, *Neighbours* or *Home and Away*, but issues which these television programmes omit are needed to complete the picture. There is little reference to politics or religion in popular entertainment, and it is these which are fundamental to personal identity and are more enduring than fashions in clothes or music. Certainly any accurate prediction about the future values and religious beliefs of the next generation of adults would do well to examine what teenagers today think and believe. That is what this survey into teenage religion and values today sets out to do.

The Survey Population

We set out to profile young people in state maintained schools. Government figures given in *Social Trends 23* (1993, table 3.7 and page 40) show that 93% of the nation's school-age young people are educated in this way. Overall there are slightly more than 3 million young people in state maintained secondary education in England and Wales. Of these, over 2.8 million pupils are in England and over 0.1 million in Wales. Such figures exclude the relatively small number of pupils in special schools.

The sample was taken from pupils in years nine and ten, that is, young people aged between 13 and 15 years. There are two reasons for this: first, these pupils are at a point of transition between childhood and adulthood, which was the focus of the study, and second, by concentrating on two year groups, we were able to compare figures for year nine and ten pupils and detect any trend in shifts of opinion.

The sample included pupils from different ethnic and religious backgrounds. However, because we were interested in a Christian model of religious belief and, at the same time, wanted to compare large or relatively similar sized groups with each other, we left out of the analysis reported here pupils who belonged to non-Christian faith communities, for example those who identified themselves as being Buddhist, Islamic, Jewish, Hindu, Mormon, Hari Krishna or Jehovah's Witness. We hope to turn attention to some of these groups in subsequent publications.

The sample is large. It amounts to the size of a small town. Altogether just over 13,000 young people completed the questionnaires utilised in the present analysis. A sample of this size allows us to generalise with some confidence to the population as a whole.

Standing behind all the percentages quoted in this book are real people. There are approximately half a million year nine and half a million year ten pupils in England and Wales (*Annual Abstract of Statistics 1994*, table 5.2 and page 88). Therefore, assuming that this sample accurately reflects the population from which it is drawn, 1% of the sample represents about 10,000 individuals in England and Wales. This means that 5% of the sample represents 50,000 and 40% of the sample represents 400,000. To take a more or less arbitrary example reported in the text, 62% of pupils say they are worried about getting AIDS; consequently this should be understood to show that approximately 620,000 year nine and ten teenagers are troubled by this worry. Looked at in this way the percentage figures take on a greater significance.

The issues presented to pupils

Pupils were given a substantial questionnaire and invited to complete it anonymously and confidentially during school time. All the items in the questionnaire were in the form of simple statements which pupils could easily understand. To each statement pupils responded by agreement, uncertainty or disagreement. The statements themselves were in a random order so that, for example, the references to school or to sexual morality were separated from each other and not blocked into consecutive items. This arrangement makes it much more difficult for pupils to impose an artificial pattern on their responses or to make their attitudes and values appear more organised than is in fact the case.

The questionnaire has a well-established pedigree. In 1984 Leslie Francis published *Teenagers and the Church* (Collins), which presented data derived from a specially developed questionnaire whose prototype was the *Centymca Attitude Inventory*, which had been used on studies dating back to the late 1970s. The questionnaire presented to pupils in this study made use of the experience and expertise gained in the previous studies. Items had been compiled after listening carefully to young people's views on the issues under examination. Moreover, in order to gain an exact comparison between these issues, items were frequently put into statements with the same stem: 'I am worried about...' or 'It is wrong to...'. This careful procedure also allows comparisons to be made with earlier samples and other surveys.

For the purposes of analysis statements on similar themes were drawn together. These themes have become the different chapters of this book.

Chapter 2, *Listening ear*, is concerned with the need that young people have for someone with whom to talk about their problems. How many young people feel the need for a confidant? How many young people can talk to their parents, or prefer to talk to their mother rather than to their father? How many young people prefer to talk to friends rather than to either parent? Are the caring professions (ministers, doctors, teachers, social workers and youth club leaders) seen as being equally approachable and helpful?

Chapter 3, *School*, focuses attention on broad perspectives connected with the process of education. Are pupils happy at school and, if they are, is this because they like the company of their friends rather than the teachers or the subjects they are taught? How many pupils are frightened of being bullied? How many pupils think school is really preparing them for the life ahead? Is school plain boring?

Chapter 4, *Well-being,* is concerned with how young people feel about themselves. Do young people think life is worth living? Do they feel they are, as people, worth much? Are they fundamentally lonely? Or do they have a sense of purpose in their lives? Are there many young people who are depressed? How many young people have contemplated suicide?

Chapter 5, *My area,* concentrates on the neighbourhood where young people live. Are young people satisfied with the shopping facilities which are provided? Do they like the area overall? Do they feel their area actually cares about the young? Do they see a growth in vandalism, crime and drunkenness? Is drug-taking on the increase? And what about unemployment? Is it growing?

Chapter 6, *Concerns,* approaches large general topics about which young people might feel unease. Do young people feel that nuclear war is a threat? Is pollution or Third World poverty more likely to trouble them? Is television violence a real cause for concern? How many young people are concerned about pornography? In the end, do they feel they can do anything to solve the world's problems?

Chapter 7, *Sexual morality*, samples teenagers' views on the rights and wrongs of different kinds of sexual behaviour. Do teenagers think it is wrong to have sexual intercourse outside marriage? Do they think it is wrong to have sexual intercourse under the legal age (16 years)? Are abortion, contraception and divorce right or wrong?

Chapter 8, *Right and wrong*, engages with typical moral topics, but excludes those to do with sex. It is concerned with down-to-earth practical matters. How many pupils think there is anything wrong with shop-lifting, or travelling on public transport without a ticket, or buying alcohol or cigarettes under age? Is writing graffiti generally thought to be all right? Do the police do a good job? Is playing truant actually wrong? What about riding a bicycle without lights at night?

Chapter 9, *Substance use*, focuses on the rights and wrongs of taking substances which may be harmful, including glue, marijuana, alcohol, butane gas, cigarettes and heroin. Which of these substances do most pupils think it is wrong to take? Do any pupils see nothing wrong in taking all of them? Is alcohol thought to be more harmful than nicotine, or vice versa?

Chapter 10, *Leisure,* relates leisure to home and friends. It does not list a set of sporting activities to see which is the most popular. Instead it finds out if the Youth Centre is boring or if parents approve of their teenagers' use of leisure time. Do young people wish they had more things to do? Do they often hang around with their friends doing nothing in particular? Are they frightened of going to the Youth Centre? Do their parents want them out of the house?

Chapter 11, *Religious beliefs*, looks mainly at beliefs associated with Christianity. How many pupils believe that Jesus is the Son of God or that he rose literally from the dead? Do they, indeed, believe in God? Do they believe God made the world in six days? Is Christianity the only true religion and does God punish those who do wrong? Is there life after death?

Chapter 12, *Supernatural,* is about the beliefs of young people in the supernatural as a whole. Do young people, in any numbers, believe in black magic or in the possibility of contacting the spirits of the dead? Do they believe in their horoscopes or fortune-tellers? Would they be frightened of going into a church alone or a graveyard alone? Do they believe in the devil?

Chapter 13, *Worries,* finds out what young people are really worried about. How many young people are worried about getting AIDS? Do they worry about going out alone at night or being attacked by pupils from other schools? Are they worried about their sex lives or about their attractiveness to the opposite sex? Are they simply worried about how they get on with others?

Chapter 14, *Work,* explores young people's views about employment and youth training. Would young people rather be unemployed than on a youth training course? Do they think youth training offers useful skills? Would they prefer unemployment to an unenjoyable job? Do they think a job brings with it a sense of purpose? Do they think most unemployed people could really get a job if they tried?

Chapter 15, *Church and society*, looks at some of the ways young people see the church as functioning in society. Do young people want to be married in church or have their own children baptised/christened? Does church simply seem irrelevant to modern life? Is church boring? Do Christian ministers do a good job? Should religious education be taught in school? What do young people think about assembly? As a daily activity, should it take place?

Chapter 16, *Politics*, discovers what young people think about local and national politics. Do young people have confidence in the main political parties? Are they sceptical about the whole process and think that it does not matter which party is in power? Do they think the local council does a good job? Do they think immigration to Britain should be restricted or that private medicine should be abolished? Is nationalisation a good thing? Do the Trade Unions have too much power? Would young people abolish private schools?

The structure of each chapter

Each chapter has a similar format. The items used in the composition of the chapter are introduced and then an overview using the whole sample of pupils is given and the main findings presented. After this, comparisons are drawn between different sub-groups of the sample.

First, males and females are compared. This is because many of the issues will be viewed from different perspectives by the two sexes and because of the known differences in male and female church attendance which are relevant to a later section of the analysis. Then a comparison between year nine and year ten pupils is drawn to allow for the detection of any age trends.

The next sets of comparisons explore the effects of religion on young people. We conceptualise religion in three ways: according to *practice* (churchgoing), *belief* (in God) and *belonging* (denominational allegiance). We examine the effects of churchgoing to see whether three groups, defined as weekly attenders, occasional attenders and non-attenders, are different from each other. Then we classify all non-churchgoing pupils into three categories on the basis of their response to the statement, 'I believe in God'. Those who agree that they believe are designated 'theists', those who are uncertain are designated 'agnostics' and those who disagree are designated 'atheists'. The purpose of this comparison is to see what difference belief in God or lack of it, without the institutional support of the church, makes to pupils' views. After this we compare weekly churchgoers in Anglican, Roman Catholic and Free Church settings to see how and if their views differ.

As a consequence of this structure each chapter is supported by a set of six tables. The first table in each set provides a full overview of the attitudes of young people in general. In relation to each statement this overview provides three pieces of information: the proportion of young people who agree with the statement, the proportion of young people who disagree with the statement, and the proportion of young people who are uncertain about their position. The other five tables in each set present the following comparisons: the responses of male and female teenagers; the responses of year nine and year ten pupils; the responses of young people who attend church weekly, who attend church less frequently than this and who never attend church; the responses of young people who never attend church but believe in God, who never attend church and do not believe in God, and who never attend church and regard themselves as agnostics; the responses of regular churchgoers who attend the Catholic Church, the Anglican Church, or one of the Free Churches. In all of these tables, the statistics illustrate the proportions of young people who agree with the statements. Although these tables do not present the proportions of young people who disagree with the statements or who express uncertainty about them, these additional statistics are provided in the narrative of the text wherever such additional information would be helpful.

At the end of each chapter, we draw out implications, some practical and some theoretical, from the data, including both the overview statistics and the comparisons which have been made according to age, sex and religion.

In the interests of simplicity we have made use of percentages throughout this study so that all those who are professionally and personally interested in the young, but who lack an understanding of multivariate statistical analysis, can follow the discussion. Those who wish for more sophisticated and technical analyses will find them in future publications arising from this database.

Sub-groups within the survey

Of the whole sample of approximately 13,000 pupils from 65 schools in different parts of England and Wales, 49% are male and 51% female. The sample is made up of 53% of year nine pupils and 47% of year ten pupils; the lower percentage of year ten pupils probably reflects the higher truancy rates at this age (as, for example, reported by the University of North London's Truancy Unit) and the demands of examination work. This does not affect the comparisons between these year groups, but it does mean that, on those issues in which there is a shift in opinion with age (usually in a more liberal direction), the reported overall figure will be marginally more conservative than should be the case. However, for all practical purposes this distinction is very slight indeed.

Of the 65 schools which contributed pupils to the sample, 57 were county schools, 2 were Church of England aided schools and 6 were Roman Catholic aided schools. Calculating on the number of schools, therefore, 9.2% of the sample is Roman Catholic and 3% Anglican. National figures show that 9.7% of secondary schools are Roman Catholic (excluding special agreement and self-governing schools) and 4.1% are Anglican (with the same exclusions). There is therefore a good match between the shape of the sample of schools and the national profile.

What the survey reported here is not able to assess is the number of pupils who were playing truant on the day when the questionnaire was filled in. Government tables of truancy rates have been subjected to fierce criticism, partly because the criteria used to define truancy have been flexibly interpreted. It is not easy to give an estimate of the number of pupils who might be expected to be absent from school on any one day. What can be assumed, however, is that the pupils who were absent from school on the day when the questionnaire was completed would be *more* likely to support truancy, petty crime and drugs than those who were present. This survey is therefore likely to underestimate the number of pupils who think there is nothing wrong with these activities.

When the whole sample is divided by church attendance, the figures show that 54% of pupils never attend church, 35% are occasional attenders and 11% are weekly attenders. Brierley (1991) gives 9.5% of the total adult population of England as attending church and 13.7% of the child population as attending (where a child is defined as being under 14 years of age). Since this sample covers 13 to 15 year olds, a figure of 11% for church attenders is consistent with Brierley's findings.

When the 11% of the sample who are weekly church attenders are examined in greater detail, 36% of this subgroup of the whole sample are found to be Anglican, 37% to be Roman Catholic and 27% to belong to the Free Churches. When the 54% of the sample who do not attend church or belong to another religious group are examined in greater detail, the subdivision into theists, agnostics and atheists shows that, of this subgroup of the total sample, 23% are theists, 37% are agnostics and 40% are atheists.

When the sex ratios are examined, non-churchgoing theists are slightly more inclined to be female (51% as against 49%), and the same applies to non-churchgoing agnostics (also 51% as against 49%). Non-churchgoing atheists, however, are much more inclined to be male (63% as against 37%) which means that male atheists outnumber female atheists by a figure approaching 2:1. In the comparisons which follow throughout this book this explains why atheists have a profile closer to that of boys than to that of girls. It also means that differences between theists and agnostics are much more likely to be as a result of this stance towards God and not to be an artifact of sex differences.

A similar set of findings is displayed with regard to church attendance. The sex ratios show that non-attenders are more likely to be male (55% are boys and 45% girls) and that weekly attenders are more likely to be female (63% are girls and 37% boys). Occasional attenders are intermediate (44% are boys and 56% girls). When comparisons are made, therefore, in each chapter of this book between weekly, occasional and non-attenders at church, it comes as no surprise that the profile of opinions held by weekly church attenders is closer to that of girls in general than to boys in general.

Cross-references and parallel work

The database assembled as a result of our survey has generated the information presented in this book. Space does not permit a detailed dialogue with surveys and databases carried out and compiled by other researchers working in overlapping and related fields. Such a dialogue has certainly begun and recent papers by Francis and Mullen (1993) and Francis and Jones (1994) demonstrate the possibility of fruitfulness. Nonetheless it is helpful to check how our study fits in with work being done elsewhere. Surveys of national significance in health education and in sexual behaviour and attitudes include comparable markers.

The Schools Health Education Unit based at Exeter University surveyed 20,218 pupils in years seven to ten in 1992, and of these 2,473 were in year nine and 8,602 in year ten, a total of 11,075. Some of the questions asked in the current survey are similar to those asked by the Schools Health Education Unit and referred to in *Young People in 1992* (Balding, 1993). This makes it convenient to see whether the results of these two surveys agree. If they do, then the sampling procedures adopted by both can be treated with even greater confidence.

Both surveys used 'opportunity samples' in the sense that neither was a national survey making use of strictly random procedures in the selection of respondents. Yet Balding (1993) was able to show that a sample of 50 pupils of each sex in a very large year group of 450 individuals gives a reliable reflection of the total population for most questions. Where the year group is smaller, as is usually the case, a sample of 100 from any year group is more than adequate, particularly if it is administered in non-streamed time.

This survey on teenage religion and values took, on average, 200 pupils, roughly half of whom were in year nine and half in year ten, from each of the 65 participating schools. Indeed, the research instructions given to staff asked them to make sure that *all* (original emphasis) their year nine and year ten pupils were surveyed.

One of the questions addressed by the Schools Health Education Unit was, 'If you wanted to share family problems, to whom would you probably turn?' and it gave a set of possible confidants: mother, father, both parents, sibling, relation, teacher, friend, employer or no one. In a similar fashion our survey contained the three separate items, 'I find it helpful to talk about my problems with my mother', 'I find it helpful to talk about my problems with my father' and 'I find it helpful to talk about my problems with close friends'. The Schools Health Education Unit discovered (page 116) that young people preferred to talk to their friends (and girls were twice as likely to do this as boys) and that, after this, both parents would be approached. If, however, only one parent was chosen, mothers were about four times as likely as fathers to be selected. This survey (as chapter two shows in detail) found a similar order of preferences. It was 61% of young people who agreed that they would find it helpful to talk to close friends, and this was followed by 51% who agreed they would go to their mothers and only 31% who would find it helpful to talk to their fathers. Moreover, the age trend in both surveys was the same. Friends became more important and parents less important as pupils passed from year nine to year ten.

To take another example, the Schools Health Education Unit asked, 'What do you know about these drugs?' and then listed the percentage of pupils who said that particular drugs were 'always unsafe' (see page 68). The most unsafe drugs, according to both boys and girls in year ten, were solvents, followed closely by heroin. Cannabis leaf and resin were thought to be unsafe by about 40% of girls and boys, that is, about two-thirds of those who thought that heroin and solvents were always unsafe. In our survey pupils were given these three statements, 'It is wrong to sniff glue', 'It is wrong to use marijuana (hash or pot)' and 'It is wrong to use heroin'. Again, it was glue (or solvents) which were agreed to be wrong by the largest percentage of pupils, followed closely by heroin. A little over two-thirds of the percentage who thought glue was wrong, made the same judgement about marijuana (which is a form of cannabis). Thus the findings of the two surveys coincided.

Another important survey bears comparison with the research reported here. Wellings *et al* (1994) used a large multi-stage sampling frame stratified by the socio-economic characteristics of the neighbourhood within Registrar General's Standard Regions. This led them to interview 18,876 randomly selected people throughout Britain aged between 16 and 59 by first randomly selecting the area and then, by using a post-code, an address within that area. Once the address was chosen, an individual living at the address was randomly selected and asked to take part. The procedure, however, made it more likely that people living alone would be asked to take part than people living in large households. Moreover it ignores the homeless and some of those living in institutions. There were also complications caused by different response rates in rural and urban regions. These deficiencies were corrected by weighting the data according to a 'product of the regional weight and the household size weight scaled on the actual sample size'. All in all this was a major piece of work, carried out to international standards of accuracy and sophistication at a cost of approximately £1 million.

Wellings *et al* found that 37.7% of women think abortion to be always or mostly wrong, compared with 33.1% of men, and that 'generally speaking, younger people are less sympathetic than older people towards abortion, though the differences are not marked.' The figures quoted by Wellings *et al* relate to their entire sample covering the full age range. The sample reported here, of course, though smaller, only deals with an age range between 13 and 15. Our findings show that 42% of girls, compared with 33% of boys, hold abortion to be wrong. This makes the match between the two surveys striking.

There is one further finding which is worth underlining. This concerns the effects of religion on sexual behaviour. In each chapter the report of our survey explores the effects of denominational settings on young people's beliefs. Wellings *et al* asked about the age of first sexual intercourse. They say, 'those reporting no religious affiliation were more likely to experience intercourse before the age of 16, and the differences are more marked for women than men. Respondents belonging to the Church of England or other Christian religions (excluding Roman Catholic) were less likely to experience sexual intercourse before the age of 16.... More surprisingly perhaps, given the position of the Roman Catholic Church on sexual behaviour, those reporting Roman Catholic affiliation are no less likely than those reporting another religious affiliation to report intercourse before the age of 16, and if anything slightly more so' (p 55). Their figures show that 13.4% of Anglican males report first sexual intercourse before 16, and that this compares with 14.6% of other Christian groups and 19.5% of Roman Catholics. Our survey also showed that Roman Catholics stood apart from Anglican and Free Church attenders on the matter of sexual intercourse under the age of 16. Whereas 47% of Free Church attenders and 41% of Anglicans believe that it is wrong to have sexual intercourse under 16 years of age, the comparable figure for Roman Catholics is 32%. Given that there is a connection between not believing something to be wrong and practising it, the two surveys point in the same unexpected direction. This, then, consolidates the validity of the church attendance variable in our survey both in terms of the sample on which it is based and in its applicability to teenage attitudes.

References

Balding, J (1993), *Young People in 1992*, University of Exeter, Schools Health Education Unit.

Brierley, P (1991), *'Christian' England*, London, Marc Europe.

Francis, L J and Jones, S H (1994), The relationship between Eysenck's personality factors and fear of bullying among 13–15 year olds in England and Wales, *Evaluation and Research in Education* (in press).

Francis, L J and Mullen, K (1993), Religiosity and attitudes towards drug use among 13–15 year olds in England, *Addiction*, 88, 665–672.

Wellings, K, Field, J, Johnson, A M and Wadsworth, J (1994), *Sexual Behaviour in Britain*, Harmondsworth, Penguin.

2   Listening ear

Introduction

In this chapter we describe the need of young people for a 'listening ear'. To sample the extent of this need we put forward nine specific statements. The first said, 'I often long for someone to turn to for advice'. By looking at the distribution of responses to this statement we could quickly see how widespread was the sense of longing for a confidant. We designed the next five statements to find out how ready teenagers are to talk to caring professionals with whom they may come into contact. The statements concern school teachers, youth club or group leaders, doctors, Christian ministers, vicars or priests and social workers. Then three statements were focused on mother, father and friends.

Overview

The survey results show that just over a third (35%) of 13 to 15 year old teenagers long for someone to turn to for advice. An almost equal proportion (39%), however, feel no such need. In the middle are the 26% who are uncertain about how to respond.

Table 2.1   Listening ear: overview

	Agree %	Not certain %	Disagree %
I often long for someone to turn to for advice	35	26	39
I would be reluctant to discuss my problems:			
with a school teacher	46	28	26
with a youth club/group leader	48	30	22
with a doctor	32	34	34
with a Christian minister/vicar/priest	41	33	26
with a social worker	40	37	23
I find it helpful to talk about my problems:			
with my mother	51	19	30
with my father	31	23	46
with close friends	61	20	19

The most popular avenue of help comes from friendship. Sixty-one percent of 13 to 15 year olds find it helpful to talk to their friends. But, within the home, 51% find it helpful to talk to their mothers and this figure contrasts with the 31% who find it helpful to talk to their fathers. Clearly the mother is the most approachable and sympathetic person within the household. Even when the figures are viewed from a reverse perspective they tell the same story. Only 19% of young people do not find it helpful to talk to their friends, as compared with 30% who do not find it helpful to talk to their mothers. Nearly half of these teenagers (46%) found their fathers unsympathetic.

Fathers, on balance, are less approachable than the local doctor. Of the professional carers the doctor is the most approachable, whether the figures are viewed in terms of those who are reluctant to talk or those who are not reluctant to talk. Nearly a third (32%) of teenagers would be reluctant to talk with their doctor, and nearly the same number (34%) would be happy to do so. On the other hand, while nearly the same number of teenagers would find it helpful to talk to their fathers (31%), nearly half (46%) would not do so. Between 12 and 14% of teenagers therefore find fathers *less* approachable than doctors.

If the professional carers are arranged in order of approachability, the figures show that 34% of teenagers would not be reluctant to talk to their doctor, 26% would not be reluctant to talk to a school teacher or a Christian minister, vicar or priest, 23% would not be reluctant to talk to a social worker and 22% would not be reluctant to talk to a youth club/group leader. The doctor is clearly the most likely confidant and the youth club/group leader the least likely. Viewed from the reverse perspective, the order of preference does not change. The highest number of those who would be reluctant to talk about personal problems is associated with youth club/group leaders (48%) and in descending order of reluctance the figures give school teachers (46%), Christian ministers, vicars or priests (41%), social workers (40%) and doctors (32%). We discuss the implications of these findings at the end of the chapter.

If the figures for uncertainty are arranged, the order changes, but what it appears to show is that teenagers are less uncertain about those they know best. Only 19% of teenagers are uncertain about talking to their mother, 20% to their friends and 23% to their fathers. Regarding the professionals, only 28% of teenagers are uncertain about their teachers, 30% about youth club/group leaders, 33% about Christian ministers, 34% about doctors and 37% about social workers.

Does gender make a difference?

In general the figures show that girls are more likely than boys to look for a confidant and that girls find it most helpful to talk to their friends about their problems. Whereas 41% of girls long for someone to turn to for advice, the comparable figure for boys is 29%; whereas 78% of girls find it helpful to talk to their friends about their problems, the comparable figure for boys is 45%. When the reverse perspective is used, the findings are similar. Whereas 38% of girls do not look for a confidant, the same is true of 41% of boys; while only 11% of girls find it unhelpful to talk to friends about problems, the corresponding figure for boys is more than double this (27%).

In the home the mother is perceived as far more likely to be sympathetic than the father. Both sexes would prefer to talk to the mother and, although more boys than girls find their fathers helpful, the mother is still clearly the family's main confidant. The figures are: 43% of boys find their mothers helpful, as compared with 58% of girls; 39% of boys find their fathers helpful, as compared with 23% of girls. The reverse perspective shows that more than half of the girls (56%) find their fathers positively unhelpful, as compared with 36% of boys, and 26% of girls find their mothers unhelpful, as compared with 34% of boys.

Between a fifth and a quarter of both sexes (25% of boys, 21% of girls) are uncertain about whether their fathers would be helpful. Only 16% of girls are uncertain about their mothers, compared with 23% of boys.

Table 2.2   Listening ear: by gender

	Male %	Female %
I often long for someone to turn to for advice	29	41
I would be reluctant to discuss my problems:		
with a school teacher	46	45
with a youth club/group leader	50	47
with a doctor	32	33
with a Christian minister/vicar/priest	42	41
with a social worker	44	37
I find it helpful to talk about my problems:		
with my mother	43	58
with my father	39	23
with close friends	45	78

Sex differences in the perception of the caring professions are slight. Looking at the percentages of pupils reluctant to discuss their problems with various caring professions, it is clear that both girls and boys find doctors most sympathetic (boys 32% and girls 33%). Boys are more likely to judge a Christian minister as the next most approachable (boys 42%, girls 41%), whereas girls consider that a social worker is likely to be the next most sympathetic person (girls 37%, boys 44%). The sexes agree that after this come teachers (boys 46%, girls 45%) and youth leaders (boys 50% and girls 47%).

Even when the reverse perspective is used, the rank order of preference about the caring professions remains almost exactly the same. Approximately a third of boys (35%) and girls (33%) would not be reluctant to discuss their problems with a doctor; rather fewer feel the same way about teachers (boys 27%, girls 26%), ministers (boys 26%, girls 25%), social workers (boys 21%, girls 25%) and youth group/club leaders (boys 21%, girls 22%).

Does age make a difference?

The age trend shows a slight drift away from the home and the caring professions to a preference for the advice of friends. Whereas 53% of year nine pupils find it helpful to talk to their mothers, the figure drops to 48% by year ten; whereas 32% of year nine pupils find it helpful to talk to their father, the figure drops to 29% by year ten; whereas 40% of year nine pupils would be reluctant to talk to a Christian minister, the figure rises to 43% by year ten; whereas 40% of year nine pupils would be reluctant to talk to a social worker, the figure rises to 41% by year ten; whereas 45% of year nine pupils are reluctant to talk with a teacher, the figure rises to 48% by year ten; whereas 47% of year nine pupils are reluctant to talk to a youth club/group leader, the figure rises to 50% by year ten. Only doctors stand out against this trend. The same number of year ten pupils as year nine pupils would be reluctant to speak to them (33%). Friends, however, become more important: 61% of year nine pupils find it helpful to talk to friends, and this figure rises to 63% by year ten.

Table 2.3   Listening ear: by age

	Year 9 %	Year 10 %
I often long for someone to turn to for advice	35	35
I would be reluctant to discuss my problems:		
with a school teacher	45	48
with a youth club/leader	47	50
with a doctor	33	33
with a Christian minister/vicar/priest	40	43
with a social worker	40	41
I find it helpful to talk about my problems:		
with my mother	53	48
with my father	32	29
with close friends	61	63

The reverse perspective broadly confirms these findings. Slightly more year ten pupils than year nine pupils find their mothers unhelpful (32% against 28%), and the same is true for fathers (48% against 45%). With regard to Christian ministers the percentage of year nine pupils who would not be reluctant to discuss personal problems falls by year ten (26% against 25%), and similarly with respect to social workers (24% against 22%) and youth club/group leaders (23% against 21%). Teachers hold their own in the age trend because the same percentage (26%) of year nine and year ten pupils would be willing to discuss personal problems with them. Only doctors become *more* popular. Whereas 32% of year nine pupils would not be reluctant to discuss personal problems, this figure rises to 35% by year ten.

The uncertainty figures do not change by more than 3% between years nine and ten. Overall pupils are slightly less uncertain in year ten than in year nine.

Does church attendance make a difference?

In order to answer this question we explore the concern for a 'listening ear' held by three distinct groups: those who never attend church, those who attend sometimes and those who attend nearly every week. The statistics show that churchgoers are more likely than non-churchgoers to want someone to turn to for advice and that they find this advice by turning to their mothers and their friends.

Table 2.4   Listening ear: by church attendance

	Weekly %	Sometimes %	Never %
I often long for someone to turn to for advice	39	38	33
I would be reluctant to discuss my problems:			
with a school teacher	45	48	45
with a youth club/group leader	48	51	47
with a doctor	34	33	32
with a Christian minister/vicar/priest	35	42	42
with a social worker	40	40	40
I find it helpful to talk about my problems:			
with my mother	54	54	48
with my father	31	32	30
with close friends	67	64	59

In detail the statistics show that 39% of weekly church-goers long to turn to someone for advice, as compared with 38% of occasional attenders and 33% of non-attenders. Reversing the perspective gives similar results: whereas 38% of both weekly and occasional attenders do not look for someone to turn to for advice, the figure for non-attenders is higher, at 40%.

Friends to confide in are more important to churchgoers than to non-attenders. While 67% of weekly attenders and 64% of occasional attenders find it helpful to talk to friends, the figure drops to 59% for non-attenders. The reverse perspective underlines this finding. Whereas 15% of weekly attenders and 17% of occasional attenders do not find it helpful to talk to friends, the figure for non-attenders rises to 20%.

Within the family both churchgoers and non-churchgoers find the mother more helpful than the father. What is notice-able, however, is that the mother is more popular among churchgoers while the popularity of the father as a confidant is completely independent of whether the teenager is a churchgoer or not. The figures show that 54% of both weekly and occasional churchgoers find their mothers helpful, compared with 48% of non-churchgoers; conversely 28% of both weekly and occasional churchgoers do not find their mothers helpful, compared with 32% of non-church-goers. Fathers are helpful to 31% of weekly churchgoers, 32% of occasional churchgoers and 30% of non-attenders. Conversely 47% of both churchgoers and non-attenders do not find their fathers helpful, compared with 44% of occasional attenders.

Among the caring professionals, we examine the clergy first to discover the extent to which church attendance alters teenage perception of their approachability. While 35% of weekly church attenders would be reluctant to discuss personal problems with a member of the clergy, the figures rise to 42% among occasional church attenders and non-attenders. When the perspective is reversed, the figures show that 35% of weekly attenders would not be reluctant to discuss their problems with clergy, as compared with 24% of occasional attenders and 25% of non-attenders.

With regard to the other caring professions, churchgoing seems to make little difference to teenage perceptions. Almost the same percentages of weekly churchgoers, occasional churchgoers and non-attenders would be reluctant to discuss personal problems with a doctor (34%, 33% and 32% respectively) and exactly the same percentage (40%) of these three groups of teenagers would be reluctant to discuss their problems with a social worker. The figures relating to school teachers and youth club/group leaders do not vary by more than 5%, and no pattern emerges.

Uncertainty figures do not vary by more than 4% between the three groups with regard to any individual statement.

Does belief in God make a difference?

We now turn the analysis on those who do not go to church and make a comparison between three groups: 'theists' who believe in God, 'agnostics' who are uncertain about belief in God, and 'atheists' who do not believe in God at all. The statistics show that theists and agnostics are more likely to want to turn to someone for advice than are atheists, and that atheists would be more reluctant than the others to discuss their personal problems with members of the clergy.

Whereas 29% of atheists often long to turn to someone for advice, 34% of agnostics and 37% of theists have the same longing. The reverse perspective confirms that atheists are less likely to want advice: 44% of them positively do not want to turn to anybody, as compared with 37% of agnostics and 38% of theists.

As before, however, it is the mother who is the most sympathetic listener. Well over half of theists (56%) will talk to their mothers, as compared with 48% of agnostics and 42% of atheists. The trend is confirmed by the reverse perspective: the lowest percentage of those who do not find mothers helpful belongs to theists (27%), and the next lowest belongs to agnostics (30%); as many as 38% of atheists do not find it helpful to talk to their mothers.

Table 2.5   Listening ear: by belief among non-churchgoers

	Theist %	Agnostic %	Atheist %
I often long for someone to turn to for advice	37	34	29
I would be reluctant to discuss my problems:			
with a school teacher	45	45	46
with a youth club/group leader	48	44	48
with a doctor	35	31	33
with a Christian minister/vicar/priest	37	38	50
with a social worker	42	38	42
I find it helpful to talk about my problems:			
with my mother	56	48	42
with my father	33	28	29
with close friends	62	61	55

Fathers are not thought to be nearly as helpful as mothers by all three groups. While 33% of theists find fathers helpful, 47% do not. Similarly while 28% of agnostics find fathers helpful, 45% do not. While 29% of atheists find fathers helpful, 50% do not. Overall theists seem to have the most fruitful relationship with their fathers and atheists the least.

Because the family's help and support are limited, teenagers turn to each other. Sixty-two percent of theists find friends helpful, and this compares with 61% of agnostics and 55% of atheists. The reverse perspective does not give quite such a sharp picture. A fifth (20%) of theists do not find friends helpful, but 17% of agnostics take the same view, compared with 24% of atheists.

Doctors continue to be the most popular of the caring professions for all three groups. Little more than a third would be reluctant to discuss problems with a doctor (35% of theists, 31% of agnostics and 33% of atheists) and little more than a third of all three groups would not be reluctant to discuss their problems with a doctor (33% of theists, 31% of agnostics and 36% of atheists). Clergy are a little less popular than this, especially among atheists. Whereas 37% of theists and 38% of agnostics would be reluctant to discuss personal problems with the clergy, the figure rises to 50% among atheists. Conversely 27% of theists would be willing to discuss their problems with clergy, as compared with 22% of agnostics and 26% of atheists.

The other caring professions, teachers, youth club/group leaders and social workers, are treated fairly similarly by all three groups. Social workers are the least unpopular, though 42% of theists and atheists would be reluctant to discuss personal problems with them, as compared with 38% of agnostics. The proportion of theists and agnostics who would be unwilling to discuss problems with teachers runs to 45% (46% for atheists), while, for youth club/group leaders, the figures are 48% for both theists and atheists and 44% for agnostics.

Does denomination make a difference?

The previous section looked closely at young people who never attend church. Now we take a close look at those who attend weekly and explore the relationship between their denominational identity and their concern for a 'listening ear'.

Table 2.6   Listening ear: by denomination

	Catholic %	Anglican %	Free %
I often long for someone to turn to for advice	41	39	40
I would be reluctant to discuss my problems:			
with a school teacher	52	39	45
with a youth club/group leader	55	47	43
with a doctor	37	31	33
with a Christian minister/vicar/priest	44	30	32
with a social worker	42	38	40
I find it helpful to talk about my problems:			
with my mother	49	61	59
with my father	27	35	31
with close friends	66	69	73

The figures show that there is scarcely any difference between churchgoing teenagers from Roman Catholic, Anglican and Free Church backgrounds with regard to their longing for someone to turn to for advice. What the figures do highlight, however, is the relative unpopularity of Roman Catholic priests and the relative difficulty Catholic young people have in talking to their mothers. Taken overall the figures show that the Roman Catholic teenagers have most difficulty in finding a sympathetic and helpful listener.

In detail, 39% of Anglican, 40% of Free Church and 41% of Roman Catholic young people long to turn to someone for advice; reversing the perspective, 39% of Anglican, 38% of Free Church and 37% of Roman Catholic young people do not long for someone to turn to for advice. Where advice is sought, it is among friends that these churchgoers first look. Well over two-thirds of each denominational group turn to friends: 66% of Roman Catholic, 69% of Anglican and 73% of Free Church young people turn to each other. After friends, the mother remains the most popular confidant. Whereas 61% of Anglican and 59% of Free Church young people turn to their mothers, the comparable figure for Roman Catholics is significantly lower at 49%. The reverse perspective confirms this trend: 31% of Roman Catholic young people do not find it helpful to talk to their mothers, as compared with 23% of Anglican and 25% of Free Church young people.

Fathers remain less approachable than mothers. What is noticeable, however, is that, just as Anglicans found their mothers more approachable than did the other denominations, so they find their fathers more approachable. Thus 35% of Anglicans find it helpful to talk to their fathers, as compared with 31% of Free Church and 27% of Roman Catholic young people. The reverse perspective underlines these figures. Whereas over half (51%) of Roman Catholic young people find their fathers positively unhelpful, the figures for the other denominations are lower, at 48% for the Free Church and 41% for the Anglican young people.

The caring professionals are viewed very similarly by the teenagers from these three denominational groups. There is, though, one important trend in the figures. The Roman Catholic teenagers are more reluctant to discuss their problems with social workers, doctors, youth club leaders and teachers than are Christian young people from the other two denominations. Whereas 42% of Roman Catholic young people would be reluctant to discuss their problems with a social worker, the figures for Anglican and Free Church teenagers are 38% and 40% respectively; whereas 37% of Roman Catholic young people would be reluctant to discuss their problems with a doctor, the figures for Anglican and Free Church teenagers are 31% and 33% respectively; whereas 55% of Roman Catholic teenagers would be unwilling to discuss their problems with a youth club/group leader, the figures for Anglican and Free Church teenagers are 47% and 43% respectively; whereas 52% of Roman Catholic teenagers would be unwilling to discuss their problems with a school teacher, the figures for Anglican and Free Church teenagers are 39% and 45% respectively. In this respect the Free Church and Anglican young people are more similar to each other than they are to the Roman Catholic young people.

So far as the relative popularity of the caring professions is concerned, doctors *on average* are preferred above clergy, social workers, teachers and youth club/group leaders *in that order*. Nevertheless some Anglican young people prefer their clergy above doctors, though this finding is equivocal because, when the perspective is reversed, 40% of Anglican young people would be willing to discuss their problems with their clergy, as compared with 36% who would be willing to talk to their doctors. Free Church young people demonstrate a similar ambivalence. Whereas 33% of Free Church young people would be reluctant to discuss their problems with a doctor, a slightly lower number (32%) would be reluctant to discuss their problems with a minister. The reverse perspective shows an opposite preference: 38% would be willing to talk to a minister but 39% to a doctor.

The figures for the Roman Catholic young people are clear-cut whichever perspective is used; they prefer doctors to priests.

Uncertainty figures show no clear denominational trend.

Implications

More than a third (35%) of young people 'often long for someone to turn to for advice'. Despite the pastoral care and vocational guidance within schools, a significant proportion of young people feels in need of help. A more significant proportion (39%), however, claims to need no advice. Young people in the age group between 13 and 15 years are therefore divided. Some shrug off the advice of adults, while others feel in need of it. Yet, despite the 39% of young people who say they do not often long for someone to turn to, 51% of young people say they find it helpful to talk to their mothers. Because of the 12% gap between these two figures, we may be correct to deduce that some of those young people who feel they need no advice are able to take this stance because of good relationships with their mothers.

The large number of teenagers who find it helpful to talk with their mothers suggests that the mother forms the main bridge to the older generation. She is the person most likely to represent the values and opinions of the older generation to teenagers in a way that they will listen to, and she is most likely to hold the family together.

There are, nevertheless, a large group (30%) who do not find it helpful to talk to their mothers. When we add to this group the 46% who do not find it helpful to talk to their fathers, the figures suggest tension and alienation within a significant number of homes. The figures do not tell us how many of those who find their fathers unhelpful also find their mothers unhelpful, but, since we know that 35% 'often long for someone to turn to', we may be correct in assuming that a considerable number of teenagers feel alienated from both parents.

Certainly the contrast between mothers and fathers is marked. A greater number of teenagers find their fathers unhelpful (46%) than helpful (31%). Friction in the home is implied. In up to 20% of cases (that is the 51% who find mothers helpful minus the 31% who find fathers helpful) there is a possibility of tension between parents centred on relationships with the young. Where the mother finds herself having simultaneously to maintain a loving relationship with her husband and her teenage children when husband and children are antagonistic to each other, the stress which the mother, in her late 30s or early 40s, is likely to feel should give churches and social agencies cause for concern. There is surely a need for counselling about parenting skills to be more widely available.

The caring professions seem unable to command the confidence of at least half of these 13 to 15 year olds. Yet, if there is anyone they can talk to, it is the doctor. This speaks well of the discretion and professionalism of General Practitioners. Up to 68% of teenagers feel some freedom about talking to their doctors, and we may be safe to assume that people who feel able to talk about private *physical* problems will also feel able to talk about private *psychological* and emotional problems.

The obstacle faced by young people in respect of the caring professions is not to do with accessibility. After all, they see teachers every school day of the year. The obstacle must be concerned with perception. If we consider that teachers are of both sexes and that, while Christian ministers are more likely to be male, social workers are more likely to be female, the difficulty cannot be connected with the gender of the carer. Nor can it be connected with the professional or moral code of the carer to any great extent since the professional ethics of each of these groups are different. Whereas the priest or the doctor may be bound by rules of confidentiality, the teacher and the social worker are not held by such a restricted set of guidelines. Yet there is no obvious connection between professional code and popularity among the young.

Sex differences suggest that boys have more difficulty than girls in finding help. The cultural stereotype of the tongue-tied male who cannot express his feelings finds support in these figures. Up to 59% of boys may want to turn to someone for help (that is, all those boys who say they often long for advice added to those who are uncertain). The comparable figure for girls is 62%, which is fairly similar. Yet girls find help from their friends and their mothers far more often than do boys; more importantly the number of girls who find their friends helpful is *larger* than the number of girls who may long for help. This suggests that many girls find an adequate network of support within their peer group. A *smaller* number of boys finds their friends helpful than those who may long for help. This suggests that some boys may want help but be unable to get it.

Although teenage girls find help from their mothers and their friends, more than half (56%) clash with their fathers. A much lower number of boys (36%) does not find their fathers helpful. An implication for one-parent families is that girls will suffer less from the absence of a father than will boys. Yet this conclusion, while it may be true in some instances, must be treated with caution since relationships with step-parents and absent parents are likely to show significantly different patterns from those with natural parents.

The age trend displays a decreasing reliance on family and caring professions (with the exception of the doctor) and a greater tendency to turn to friends. This is especially noticeable because the percentage of young people who long for someone to turn to remains constant between year nine and year ten; what changes is the willingness to look for help from adults. Studies of the teen years which see them as a transition from dependence to independence are therefore supported by these figures.

The profile of church attenders reflects the pattern of figures for girls. This is not surprising because females are more likely than males to attend church. Church attenders are thus more likely to want someone to talk to, to have good relationships with their mothers and to find it helpful to talk to friends.

The approachability of Christian ministers is a matter of disagreement. Whereas 35% of weekly churchgoers would be reluctant to talk to their minister, 35% of weekly churchgoers would be happy to do so. These figures suggest that, at least for Anglican and Free Church teenage churchgoers, ministers are *more approachable* than any other of the caring professions, including doctors. Since skills for dealing with young people can either be learnt or improved upon it would be wise to include them as part of ministerial training.

We can only speculate about the effects of an increasing number of women vicars, priests or ministers on young people. If girls are more frequent church attenders than boys, and if girls tend to get on better with their mothers than do boys, then it is probable that some girls will form the sort of relationship with their vicar, priest or minister which they form with their mothers. What the present figures show is that a simplistic Freudian explanation of religion does not work. We might expect those who do not get on well with their fathers to find in religion a father-substitute. The figures do not support this. Weekly churchgoers and non-attenders show the same level of antipathy to their fathers, and occasional church attenders are slightly more likely than others to have a good relationship with their fathers.

Atheists demonstrate a sturdy independence in these figures. They are least likely to want to turn to someone for help and they contrast sharply with non-churchgoing theists who are most likely to want to turn to someone for advice. Yet atheists are also least likely to have good relationships with their parents. Whereas 56% of non-churchgoing theists and 48% of agnostics find their mothers helpful, the figure drops to 42% for atheists, and the reverse perspective confirms this finding. The pattern for fathers is similar. Non-churchgoing theists find their fathers more helpful than do atheists; half of atheists do not find their fathers helpful (compared with 47% of non-churchgoing theists).

These figures cannot show whether atheists become atheists because of poor family relationships or whether family relationships dispose some teenagers to reject belief in God; conversely it is impossible to say whether theists cultivate good relationships with their parents or whether good relationships with parents lead to theism.

The consistent pattern of figures shows that the difficulty of Roman Catholic teenagers in relating to their priests and parents (as compared with Anglican or Free Church young people) may be related to the obligation which children from Roman Catholic homes have to attend church. Whereas Anglican and Free Church children are more likely to be voluntary church attenders, Roman Catholic children are more liable to be pressed to attend. In this respect the sample of Roman Catholic young people may be distinct from the Anglican and Free Church sample.

3   School

Introduction

This chapter deals with young people's ideas about school. We put forward eight statements. 'I am happy in my school' and 'I like the people I go to school with' explored an emotional dimension. 'I often worry about my school work', 'I am worried about my exams at school', 'My school is helping to prepare me for life' and 'Teachers do a good job' focused on the academic and practical side of school. The items, 'I am worried about being bullied at school' and 'school is boring' tested possible reasons for dislike of school.

Overview

Most pupils (90%) like the people they go to school with and most (71%) are happy at school. More than two-thirds of teenagers (67%) think that school is preparing them for life and two out of five (42%) think that teachers are doing a good job. Most teenagers (52%) are not worried about being bullied and two out of five (42%) do not find school boring. The main and perfectly natural concerns for the majority of teenagers (62%) refer to their school work and, for nearly three-quarters (73%), the looming threat of exams.

Table 3.1   School: overview

	Agree %	Not certain %	Disagree %
I am happy at school	71	18	11
I like the people I go to school with	90	7	3
I often worry about my school work	62	17	21
School is boring	35	23	42
I am worried about my exams at school	73	14	13
I am worried about being bullied at school	25	23	52
Teachers do a good job	42	31	27
My school is helping to prepare me for life	67	21	12

In contrast with this relatively positive group of pupils must be set an unhappy minority (11%). Some feelings of unhappiness may arise because as many as 3% of pupils do not like the people they go to school with and because over a quarter (27%) do not think that teachers are doing a good job. More seriously, a quarter of pupils (25%) are worried about being bullied. The threat of violence apart, the complaint of more than a third of pupils (35%) is that schools are simply boring, and 12% feel that school is not preparing them for life.

The uncertainty figures show considerable variation. As many as 18% of pupils are not sure if they are happy in school, 7% are uncertain if they like the people they go to school with, 31% are unsure how to assess teachers and 21% cannot say if school is preparing them for life. As many as 23% of pupils are unsure if they are worried about being bullied or if school is boring and 17% do not know if they often worry about their school work. Even with respect to exams, 14% of pupils are not sure if they worry.

Does gender make a difference?

There are four main areas of difference between male and female ideas about school. First, girls are more consistently worried than boys about their exams (79%, compared with 66%), a finding confirmed by the greater number of boys (19%) than girls (9%) who are not worried about exams. Second, day-to-day school work concerns more girls (67%) than boys (58%), a finding also confirmed by the reverse perspective when 23% of boys and 17% of girls do not worry about their school work. Third, boys are more inclined to think school is boring than are girls (38% of boys, compared with 31% of girls). Put the other way, 40% of boys do not think school is boring, compared with 45% of girls. Lastly, girls are more concerned than boys about being bullied. As many as 28% of girls have a worry about being bullied, whereas the figure for boys is 22%; conversely 56% of boys are not scared of being bullied, as compared with 48% of girls.

Table 3.2   School: by gender

	Male %	Female %
I am happy at school	69	72
I like the people I go to school with	89	92
I often worry about my school work	58	67
School is boring	38	31
I am worried about my exams at school	66	79
I am worried about being bullied at school	22	28
Teachers do a good job	41	42
My school is helping to prepare me for life	68	66

Yet, despite these worries and fears, more girls consistently show a positive evaluation of school than do boys. Seventy-two per cent of girls, compared with 69% of boys, are happy at school and 92% of girls, compared with 89% of boys, like the people with whom they go to school. Both these findings are confirmed by the reverse perspective: 13% of boys, compared with 10% of girls, are not happy at school and 3% of boys, compared with 2% of girls, do not like the people with whom they go to school.

There is one further distinction between the sexes, and this relates to their assessment of teachers. While 41% of boys and 42% of girls think that teachers do a good job, the percentage of girls who evaluate teachers negatively is 23%, which is considerably lower than the 31% of boys who do so. Rather more girls (35%) than boys (28%) are uncertain how to rate teachers. The remaining statistics vary by no more than 4% between the sexes.

Does age make a difference?

The age trend of ideas about school demonstrates increasing disaffection with many aspects of school. Whereas 73% of year nine pupils say they are happy at school, the figure drops to 68% of year ten pupils; whereas 69% of year nine pupils think school is helping prepare them for life, the figure drops to 64% for year ten pupils; whereas 43% of year nine pupils think teachers do a good job, the figure drops to 40% for year ten pupils; whereas 32% of year nine pupils find school boring, the figure rises to 38% of year ten pupils. Worry about school work increases from 61% of year nine pupils to 64% of year ten pupils and there is a 1% increase in worry about exams from the 72% of year nine pupils.

Table 3.3   School: by age

	Year 9 %	Year 10 %
I am happy at school	73	68
I like the people I go to school with	90	90
I often worry about my school work	61	64
School is boring	32	38
I am worried about my exams at school	72	73
I am worried about being bullied at school	27	23
Teachers do a good job	43	40
My school is helping to prepare me for life	69	64

The reverse perspective confirms nearly all these findings. Whereas 9% of year nine pupils are unhappy at school, the figure rises to 13% of year ten pupils; whereas 11% of year nine pupils do not think that school is preparing them for life, the figure rises to 14% a year later; the figure for those who do not think teachers do a good job remains static at 27%; but the figure for pupils who do not find school boring drops from 45% in year nine to 39% in year ten and worry about academic matters also increases. Whereas 22% of year nine pupils do not worry about school work, only 19% of year ten pupils are free of this concern and the number of those who do not worry about exams drops from 14% to 13% over the year.

The only two positive changes from year nine to year ten concern a drop in worry about being bullied and a continuing appreciation of the people with whom pupils go to school; whereas 27% of year nine pupils are worried about bullying, the figure drops to 23% of year ten pupils, a finding confirmed by the reverse perspective where the increase in those who are not worried by bullying rises from

49% in year nine to 55% in year ten. Responses to the statement, 'I like the people I go to school with' remain level in all categories in the two year groups.

Does church attendance make a difference?

Considerable differences towards school are revealed by the figures between weekly churchgoers, occasional churchgoers and non-churchgoers. For example, whereas more than two out of five (41%) of non-churchgoers find school boring, the figure for occasional churchgoers is 29% and for weekly churchgoers is only a quarter (25%); whereas over three quarters of weekly churchgoers (78%) are happy in school, the figure for occasional churchgoers is 74% and for non-churchgoers is 67%; whereas more than half (52%) of weekly churchgoers think teachers do a good job, the figure for occasional churchgoers is 46% and for non-churchgoers it is 36%; likewise, whereas 72% of weekly churchgoers and 71% of occasional churchgoers think school is preparing them for life, the figure for non-churchgoers is only 63%.

Table 3.4   School: by church attendance

	Weekly %	Sometimes %	Never %
I am happy at school	78	74	67
I like the people I go to school with	90	90	90
I often worry about my school work	67	67	58
School is boring	25	29	41
I am worried about my exams at school	77	76	70
I am worried about being bullied at school	29	28	22
Teachers do a good job	52	46	36
My school is helping to prepare me for life	72	71	63

All these positive findings about churchgoers are confirmed by the reverse perspective. While 51% of weekly churchgoers do not find school boring, it is 48% of occasional churchgoers and 37% of non-churchgoers who make the same judgement; while 7% of weekly and 8% of occasional churchgoers are unhappy at school, it is 14% of non-churchgoers who admit this; while 19% of weekly churchgoers and 22% of occasional churchgoers think teachers do a good job, it is 32% of non-churchgoers who hold this opinion; while 9% of weekly and 10% of occasional churchgoers do not think school is preparing them for life, the figure for non-churchgoers is 14%.

On the other side of the coin, churchgoers are more inclined to be worried about school work and exams and to have a fear of being bullied. It is 67% of weekly and occasional churchgoers who worry about school work, as compared with 58% of non-churchgoers. It is 77% of weekly and 76% of occasional churchgoers who worry about exams, as compared with 70% of non-churchgoers. It is 29% of weekly and 28% of occasional churchgoers who are worried about being bullied, as compared with 22% of non-church- goers. Again these figures are confirmed by the reverse perspective: 17% of both weekly and occasional churchgoers do not worry about school work, compared with 24% of non-churchgoers; 10% of weekly and 12% of occasional churchgoers are unworried by exams, and this contrasts with 16% of non-churchgoers; 46% of weekly and 48% of occasional churchgoers are not worried about being bullied, and this compares with 56% of non-churchgoers who are similarly free from this problem.

The uncertainty figures vary among the three groups by no more than 4% on any of the items.

Does belief in God make a difference?

We now look in more detail at those who do not go to church and make a comparison between 'theists', 'agnos- tics', and 'atheists' (see page 7). The figures show that theists rather than atheists tend to be happier at school, not to be bored, to think that teachers are doing a good job and more inclined to think school is preparing them for life. Agnostics are usually intermediate between the two groups.

Table 3.5   School: by belief among non-churchgoers

	Theist %	Agnostic %	Atheist %
I am happy at school	72	70	60
I like the people I go to school with	91	92	88
I often worry about my school work	66	62	51
School is boring	38	38	47
I am worried about my exams at school	76	74	63
I am worried about being bullied at school	27	21	19
Teachers do a good job	44	38	30
My school is helping to prepare me for life	70	64	57

The figures give the detail. While 72% of theists and 70% of agnostics are happy at school, only 60% of atheists can say this; 38% of theists and agnostics are bored by school, but the figure for atheists is 47%; 44% of theists and 38% of agnostics think that teachers do a good job, but only 30% of atheists say this; 70% of theists and 64% of agnostics believe school is preparing them for life, but only 57% of atheists take this view. The reverse perspective confirms these figures. While 10% of theists and 11% of agnostics are unhappy at school, the figure for atheists is higher at 20%; while 42% of theists and 37% of agnostics are not bored by school, only a third of atheists (33%) can say this; while 26% of theists and 27% of agnostics do not accept that teachers are doing a good job, it is 40% of atheists who hold this opinion and, while 11% of theists and 12% of agnostics do not think school is helping to prepare them for life, a higher number of atheists (20%) shares this negative view.

The generally more favourable view of school held by theists and agnostics is accompanied by a greater tendency to worry about school work, exams and bullying. While 66% of theists and 62% of agnostics worry about school work, it is only 51% of atheists who do so. While 76% of theists and 74% of agnostics worry about exams, it is only 63% of atheists who do so and, while 27% of theists and 21% of agnostics worry about being bullied, it is 19% of atheists who do so. All these worries are confirmed by the reverse perspective: 17% of theists, 20% of agnostics and 30% of atheists do not worry about school work; 12% of both theists and agnostics and 21% of atheists do not worry about exams; 54% of both theists and agnostics and 60% of atheists do not worry about being bullied.

Does denomination make a difference?

The previous section looked at young people who never attend church. This section examines those who attend weekly, either in an Anglican, Free Church or Roman Catholic setting.

Table 3.6   School: by denomination

	Catholic %	Anglican %	Free %
I am happy at school	78	82	81
I like the people I go to school with	92	92	88
I often worry about my school work	69	67	67
School is boring	30	20	17
I am worried about my exams at school	81	77	77
I am worried about being bullied at school	29	30	34
Teachers do a good job	47	56	58
My school is helping to prepare me for life	73	75	76

The figures demonstrate that Roman Catholic pupils both tend to worry more about their school work and to be more likely to be bored by school than are teenagers of the other denominations. There is also a slightly greater tendency for Roman Catholic pupils to think that school is not preparing them for life and that teachers do not do a good job.

Thus, whereas 69% of Roman Catholic pupils worry about their school work, the figure for both Anglican and Free Church pupils is 67%; whereas 81% of Roman Catholic pupils worry about their exams, the figure for both Anglican and Free Church pupils is 77%; whereas 20% of Anglican pupils and 17% of Free Church pupils find school boring, the figure for Roman Catholic pupils rises to 30%; whereas 73% of Roman Catholic pupils think that school is preparing them for life, the figures for the other two denominational groups are slightly higher at 75% for Anglican pupils and 76% for Free Church pupils. Teachers are thought by less than half of Roman Catholic pupils (47%) to be doing a good job, compared with more than half among Anglican (56%) and Free Church pupils (58%). The reverse perspective confirms three of these findings. Less than half of Roman Catholic pupils think that school is not boring (45%) whereas the figures for Anglican and Free Church pupils are 58% and 57% respectively. Then, as many as 24% of Roman Catholic pupils fail to agree that teachers do a good job, as compared with 13% of both Anglican and Free Church pupils. Whereas 9% of Roman Catholic pupils do not think that school is preparing them for life, the figure for Anglican pupils is 7% and the figure for Free Church pupils is 4%.

One item, however, demonstrates an advantage enjoyed by Roman Catholic pupils. They are slightly but consistently less likely to worry about bullying. Whereas 34% of Free Church pupils and 30% of Anglican pupils have this worry, the figure for Roman Catholic pupils is 29%. The reverse perspective shows that 48% of Roman Catholic pupils do not worry about bullying, compared with 44% of Anglican and 41% of Free Church pupils.

Implications

Young people in overwhelming numbers enjoy the social side of school life. They like the people with whom they go to school and they describe themselves as happy at school. Their criticisms, however, fall heavily on teachers, and there must be few other professional groups whose 'customers' find fault in such large numbers. Moreover, these criticisms must contribute to the stress to which teachers are subject and of which they complain. Yet the figures suggest that young people make a distinction between what is taught and who teaches it. Although only 42% of pupils think teachers do a good job, a much higher number (67%) think that school is a useful preparation for life. The complaint here is not primarily about what is taught since two-thirds think it useful, rather it is about the *way* it is taught (35% think school is boring) and the people who do it.

The figures about bullying are alarming. We may be correct in identifying the 11% of pupils who are definitely unhappy at school as a sub-group or an overlapping group with the 25% who are worried about being bullied. Certainly there is an undercurrent of violence at school about which staff need to be alert; this is especially so since it is girls who are more likely to fear bullying. Altogether, only just over half (52%) of pupils are *not* worried about being bullied and, when we add this to the widespread concerns about school work and exams, the unhealthy face of education is revealed. Furthermore, this survey sampled pupils in the middle of their compulsory secondary education. We are entitled to ask what the figures relating to fear of bullying are lower down the school.

There are two important conclusions we can draw. First, it must be possible to reduce the fear of bullying. If we assume that most Roman Catholic pupils are taught in Roman Catholic schools, then it is legitimate to deduce that the slightly less frequent fear of bullying in Catholic schools is due partly to effective administrative and pastoral care. Second, the perception that schools prepare young people for life needs to be addressed. A third of pupils think that what they are taught is irrelevant. Their judgement in this matter may, of course, be incorrect, but at least an attempt should be made to show them how and why what is taught has a practical and future application, and if this cannot be done, there is a case for strengthening existing links between education and commerce/industry.

Sex differences show that there is less hostility to teachers among girls. While 31% of boys do not think teachers do a good job, the figure for girls is 23%. Since girls are slightly less likely than boys to think that school is preparing them for life, it is probable that girls' generally more favourable evaluation of school is informed by their enjoyment of the social relationships they form there, either with friends or with teachers. The greater anxiety about school work and exams found among girls is consistent with higher levels of anxiety found in the female population generally.

Church attenders are consistently more likely to be favourable to school. Why should this be? The data here suggest a novel explanation which needs to be more widely tested. The pattern of figures for churchgoers is very similar to the pattern of figures for theists who are not churchgoers. It may be that theism, expressed either in the context of church attendance or without the institutional support of the church, engenders an attitude to society that accepts order, purpose and authority which, in their turn, facilitate an appreciation of school. Certainly the most favourably disposed pupils towards schooling in this survey are all regular churchgoers, and this tendency is especially marked among Free Church and Anglican young people.

4 Well-being

Introduction

Well-being refers to overall mental and physical health. We implicitly refer to this concept when we say to someone, 'how do you do?' or 'how are you?' This chapter sets out teenage opinions about their personal well-being. Six topics relating to well-being were included within the survey. These are depression, suicidal thoughts, loneliness, self-worth, purpose in life and whether life is worth living. These questions are personal and direct and show, for instance, what percentage of teenagers aged 13 to 15 have sometimes considered suicide or whether there are differences between boys and girls on the matter of loneliness.

Overview

The survey reveals both good and bad news about modern teenagers. The statistics show that the majority of 13 to 15 year olds find life worth living and believe that their lives have a sense of purpose. Nearly seven out of ten (69%) teenagers agree that life is worth living and more than half (55%) believe their lives have a sense of purpose. Expressed another way, less than one teenager in ten (9%) feels that his or her life has no purpose and the same number thinks that life is not worth living. In addition nearly one teenager in three (29%) does not experience depression and 57% have never at any time considered suicide. Most teenagers in this age group (68%) would not consider themselves lonely people and nearly two teenagers out of every three (64%) reject the view that, as people, they are not worth much.

The table also shows that there is a significant minority of young people who do not take such a rosy view of themselves or of life in general. More than one in four (27%) young people have at some time considered suicide and more than half (53%) admit to feeling depressed often. More than one in ten (13%) young people admit to thinking that they are not worth much as people and nearly one young person in six (16%) tends to be lonely. To this unhappy group belong the 9% of young people who do not feel life is worth living and the 9% who feel no sense of purpose about their lives.

Table 4.1   Well-being: overview

	Agree %	Not certain %	Disagree %
I feel my life has a sense of purpose	55	36	9
I find life worth living	69	22	9
I feel I am not worth much as a person	13	23	64
I often feel depressed	53	18	29
I have sometimes considered taking my own life	27	16	57
I tend to be a lonely person	16	16	68

In the middle between the optimists and the pessimists is a group of young people who are uncertain about their own value, their sense of purpose, the value of life and even if they have considered suicide. More than one 13 to 15 year old in five (22%) are not certain if life is worth living and about the same number are not sure whether to say that they are, or are not, worth much as a person. More than one in three (36%) young people are uncertain about the sense of purpose in their lives and 18% are not sure if to say they often feel depressed. As many as 16% of these teenagers cannot say for certain if they have considered committing suicide or if they tend to be lonely. It is impossible to say if this group is cynical, 'mixed up', reserving judgement on life or liable to veer between optimism and pessimism.

Does gender make a difference?

The statistics show that there are some important differences between male and female teenagers in their attitude to aspects of well-being. In some areas girls tend to be less positive than boys. Nearly three-quarters of boys (73%) think that life is worth living, as compared with only two-thirds (66%) of girls. Only 45% of boys often feel

depressed, as compared with 60% of girls. About a quarter
of boys (24%) have considered suicide, but the figure for
girls is up to 30%. Looked at from another perspective, 60%
of boys, as compared with 54% of girls, have not considered
suicide. Only a quarter of girls (24%) do not feel depressed
often, but, for the boys, the figure is more than a third
(34%). Fewer boys doubt their self-worth (12% against 14%
of girls) and more boys (68% against 61% of girls) have
never doubted their self-worth.

Table 4.2   Well-being: by gender

	Male %	Female %
I feel my life has a sense of purpose	54	57
I find life worth living	73	66
I feel I am not worth much as a person	12	14
I often feel depressed	45	60
I have sometimes considered taking my own life	24	30
I tend to be a lonely person	17	16

In other areas girls have a more positive attitude to life
than the boys. Thus 57% of girls (only 54% of boys) think
that their lives have a sense of purpose and only 7% of girls
(but 11% of boys) think their lives do not have a sense of
purpose. Fewer girls (by only 1%, however) think that life
is not worth living (8% against 9%). When we look at the
implications of these figures at the end of this chapter we
shall comment on the fact that a sense of purpose in life
does not necessarily shield people from proneness to
depression.

In many areas, there is very little difference between the
sexes. Regarding loneliness the figures are almost the same.
Thus 16% of girls and 17% of boys consider themselves
lonely, whereas 69% of girls and 67% of boys do not make
this judgement on themselves.

The number of undecided males and females is similar.
More than a third (35% of boys and 36% of girls) cannot
decide if their life has a sense of purpose and the same

number of each sex (16%) cannot say if they have considered suicide. Almost the same percentage of males and
females in this age group (16% of boys and 15% of girls) is
not sure whether to categorise themselves as lonely. This,
perhaps, is not altogether surprising. People who enjoy their
own company do not feel alone, whereas those who have no
one to confide in may feel lonely in the hustle and bustle of
school life.

Does age make a difference?

The next table displays the effects of age on teenage well-
being. What is noticeable about these figures is that there is
hardly any shift in the percentages but where the shift does
occur, it is in the direction of less well-being.

Table 4.3   Well-being: by age

	Year 9 %	Year 10 %
I feel my life has a sense of purpose	56	54
I find life worth living	70	69
I feel I am not worth much as a person	13	13
I often feel depressed	52	53
I have sometimes considered taking my own life	26	28
I tend to be a lonely person	16	16

Whereas 56% of year nine pupils think their life has a
sense of purpose, only 54% of year ten pupils share that
opinion; at the other end of the scale 8% of year nine pupils
think their lives have no purpose, but 10% of year ten pupils
take that view. While 70% of year nine pupils think their
life is worth living, the figure has dropped to 69% by year
ten and, again, at the other end of the scale, while there are
8% of year nine pupils who dispute this view, the figure
rises to 9% a year later. Slightly more teenagers feel depressed as they grow older (53%, compared with 52%) and
a corresponding 1% drop occurs in the number who do not
feel depressed (28%, compared with 29%). The consider-

ation of suicide has only been made by 26% of year nine pupils, but by year ten, the figure rises to 28%.

In two areas, the figures are almost static. Loneliness statistics are identical in years nine and ten (16% of pupils tend to be lonely, 16% are undecided and 68% are not lonely). Self-worth remains the same so far as those who feel they have little value are concerned (13%), but there is a 1% shift (65% in year ten for 64% in year nine) among those who dispute this judgement on themselves.

Does church attendance make a difference?

If we try to explore the connection between well-being and church attendance, the figures speak to us fairly clearly. We are not entitled to deduce from them that church attendance is detrimental to mental and physical health or that only the most inadequate people are drawn into the life of a congregation. The statistics show that those who attend church weekly have a greater sense of personal well-being than those who never attend.

Table 4.4   Well-being: by church attendance

	Weekly %	Sometimes %	Never %
I feel my life has a sense of purpose	68	60	49
I find life worth living	72	70	69
I feel I am not worth much as a person	11	14	14
I often feel depressed	53	54	52
I have sometimes considered taking my own life	23	26	28
I tend to be a lonely person	18	17	16

These figures are reflected in answers to a series of questions. While 68% of weekly churchgoers feel their life has a sense of purpose, only 49% of those who never attend church feel this way; while 23% of weekly churchgoers have considered suicide, the figure for those who never attend church is 28%; while 11% of weekly churchgoers feel they are not worth much, 14% of non-churchgoers feel the same; while 72% of weekly churchgoers think life is worth living, the corresponding figure for non-churchgoers is 69%. There appear to be two exceptions to this general trend. While 52% of non-churchgoers often feel depressed, the figure for weekly churchgoers is 1% higher at 53%. This difference is almost certainly explicable by the well-known gender difference in church attendance. More females feel depressed than males and more females attend church than males. On the topic of loneliness, 18% of weekly churchgoers feel this way, but the figure for non-churchgoers is 16%.

When the figures for occasional church attendance are put alongside weekly attendance and non-attendance, they fall in the middle of the range on four of the six topics. Thus 60% of occasional churchgoers think their lives have a sense of purpose, 70% find life worth living, 26% have considered suicide and 17% tend to be lonely.

If these topics are looked at from another perspective, they tell the same story. Only 4% of weekly churchgoers think their life has no purpose, as compared with 12% of those who never attend church. Only 7% of weekly church-goers do not find life worth living, against 9% of non-attenders. Only 65% of weekly churchgoers do not feel themselves lonely people, compared with 69% of non-attenders. With regard to a consideration of suicide, church attenders are less likely to think along these lines: 63% of weekly churchgoers have never considered suicide but the figure for non-attenders is 55%. Similarly slightly more weekly churchgoers reject the view that they are not worth much (65%) than do non-attenders (64%).

Does belief in God make a difference?

Next we focus on that subgroup of teenagers who do not go to church and explore the relationship between belief in God and personal well-being. The comparison is made between three groups of non-churchgoers: the 'theists', 'agnostics' and 'atheists' (see page 7). The figures show that in three areas belief in God is a significant predictor of well-being.

Table 4.5 Well-being: by belief among non-churchgoers

	Theist %	Agnostic %	Atheist %
I feel my life has a sense of purpose	64	49	42
I find life worth living	73	69	66
I feel I am not worth much as a person	15	12	14
I often feel depressed	58	54	48
I have sometimes considered taking my own life	29	26	30
I tend to be a lonely person	16	15	17

The clearest relationship between belief in God and personal well-being concerns a sense of purpose in life. While 42% of atheists think their lives have a sense of purpose, 64% of theists think this. This difference of 22% between atheists and theists is the greatest for any of the six topics which make up the overall concept of well-being. When viewed from the reverse perspective, the figures show that only 5% of theists believe their lives have no sense of purpose compared with one in five atheists (20%). Philosophically, we should expect this, on the grounds that the atheist must assume a random origin to the universe and to human life, but the theist, by definition, believes human existence is in some sense planned and therefore purposive. Similar considerations apply to the question of whether life is worth living. While two-thirds of atheists (66%) think that their lives are worth living, the figure for theists is higher at 73%. At the other end of the scale, while 9% of theists think their lives are not worth living, the figure for atheists is higher at 11%. Moreover, theists are slightly less inclined to rate themselves as lonely people (16%) as against 17% for atheists. Again, we should not be surprised at this finding. A perception that life has a purpose and that it is worth living go naturally together.

On the other hand, theists are more inclined to experience feelings of depression than are atheists. Thus, 58% of the theists say that they often feel depressed, compared with 48% of the atheists and 54% of the agnostics. From the reverse perspective, 27% of the theists are clear that they

never feel depressed, compared with 31% of the atheists and
26% of the agnostics. The greater tendency of the theists to
feel depressed is not, however, translated into more serious
doubts of self worth or suicidal ideation. Thus, 15% of the
theists feel that they are not worth much as persons, compared with 14% of the atheists and 12% of the agnostics.
Similarly 29% of the theists say that they have sometimes
considered taking their own lives, compared with 30% of the
atheists and 26% of the agnostics.

The variability of the figures derives from the agnostic
teenagers who are not sure about their well-being. If the
level of uncertainty on each of the six topics is averaged, the
agnostics show the greatest propensity for not being able to
make up their minds. Thus, 44% of the agnostics do not
know if their life has a sense of purpose, 25% are not sure
if life is worth living, 26% are not sure of their personal
worth, 20% are not sure if they often feel depressed, 26%
are not sure if they have contemplated suicide and 17% are
not sure whether to think of themselves as lonely or not. In
general the theists are the least likely to be uncertain
(average of 19%), followed by atheists at 23% and agnostics
at 26%.

Does denomination make a difference?

This section focuses on the young people who attend church
weekly and explores the relationship between denominational identity and personal well-being within this subgroup.
The comparison is made between Roman Catholics, Anglicans and Free Church teenagers.

The statistics show that on two of the main topics in the
concept of well-being the denominations are extremely
similar. On personal worth the differences vary by less than
4%. Thus, 10% of the Roman Catholic, 11% of the Anglican
and 12% of the Free Church teenagers agree that they are
not worth much as people. Conversely 65% of both Anglicans and Roman Catholics and 67% of Free Church teenagers do not doubt their own personal worth. In the same
way, 71% of the Anglican teenagers, 73% of the Roman

Catholic teenagers and 75% of the Free Church teenagers
feel that life is worth living. Only a small group of these
teenagers does not think that life is worth living: 5% of Free
Church, 7% of Roman Catholic and 8% of Anglican weekly
churchgoers fall into this category.

Table 4.6   Well-being: by denomination

	Catholic %	Anglican %	Free %
I feel my life has a sense of purpose	67	67	73
I find life worth living	73	71	75
I feel I am not worth much as a person	10	11	12
I often feel depressed	59	54	52
I have sometimes considered taking my own life	20	25	20
I tend to be a lonely person	12	18	24

Minor differences begin to emerge on the statement concerning purpose in life. Whereas 67% of the Roman Catholic and Anglican teenagers feel that their lives have a sense
of purpose, the figure for Free Church young people rises to
73%. These differences are reflected in the uncertainty
category where the Free Church teenagers manifest least
uncertainty (24%), as compared with an Anglican uncertainty level of 29% and a Roman Catholic uncertainty level
of 30%. But the figures for denominational young people
who feel their lives definitely do not have a purpose are
small and very similar (for Free Church and Roman Catholic
it is only 3% of their teenagers and for Anglicans 4%).

The Free Church young people also register a greater
sense of being lonely than do the other two denominational
groups. Nearly a quarter of Free Church teenagers (24%)
feel themselves to be lonely. The figure for Roman
Catholics is half this and for Anglicans three quarters of this
(12% and 18% respectively). Similarly, whereas 71% of
Roman Catholics definitely do not feel lonely, the figure for
Free Church young people runs at 61%. Anglicans again fall
in the middle at 65%.

The Anglican young people show greatest variability on the matter of suicide. A quarter of Anglican young people (25%) have considered suicide at some time or other; for Free Church and Roman Catholic youth the figure is 20%. So far as those who have never considered suicide is concerned, the Anglicans show the lowest percentage. Of Roman Catholic and Free Church young people 67% have never thought about suicide, but only 60% of Anglicans claim this.

The figures on suicide are unexpected because it is the Roman Catholic young people who are more likely to say they often feel depressed. Fifty-nine percent of Roman Catholic young people often feel depressed and the corresponding figures for Anglican and Free Church teenagers are 54% and 52% respectively. The Roman Catholics also show a lower percentage of young people who claim not to feel depressed (23%), as compared with 27% of Free Church and 29% of Anglican young people.

Implications

Taking the general negative implications first, it is clear that many teenagers in the 13 to 15 year old age group are frequently unhappy. Clinically diagnosed depression affects about 25% of the adult British population at some time in their lives, and approximately 10% of adults may be suffering at any one time. Disorders of mood are found in about 15 to 20% of girls in the 15 to 19 year old age group but no comparable published estimates exist for boys (Woodroffe *et al*, 1993). Some of the young people in the present sample may have had treatment for depression, but on the day they filled in the questionnaire, each one was fit enough to attend school and capable of concentrating well enough to complete quite a long document. Yet, even so, more than half admit to being 'often' depressed.

The Office of Population Censuses and Surveys (DH2) has shown that since the mid-1970s the suicide rate for young men in England and Wales has risen steadily, whereas the rate for women has remained fairly static;

analysts have related the changes in male suicide rates to
social changes, especially increases in unemployment and
the divorce rate.

It is probable that within the group which often feels
depressed is a subgroup of the set which has considered
suicide. This smaller group probably contains the 9% who
have no sense of purpose and feel that life is not worth
living. Even if the overlap between these groups is not
perfect, we are entitled to deduce that a significant number
of young people needs help and encouragement. Suicide is
the second highest cause of death for teenagers (12%) after
road traffic accidents (61%) (Woodroffe *et al*, 1993). Suicide
prevention, which is covered by voluntary agencies like The
Samaritans as well as by alert family doctors, is best
mounted by the availability of a 'helpline' for crisis management, though there are sometimes detectable warning signs
which can prevent tragedy.

The number of suicides is completely overshadowed by
the huge number of people who deliberately harm themselves. The peak rates for suicide rise with age, but those for
self-inflicted harm are highest in the late teens and early
twenties. About 10% of those who hurt themselves in this
way are suicide attempts. While the national average for
suicides in Britain remains at about 4,000 per year, the
figure for cases of self-inflicted harm is thirty times this at
120,000 per year.

Some of the young people who have considered suicide
will not take such an irreversible step, but they will damage
themselves in some other way. Of these cases of self-
inflicted harm, 90% are self-poisonings and 50% are
accompanied by alcohol.

Teaching staff need to be aware of these dangers and
teacher training or the in-service training of teachers who are
counsellors should work out how best to integrate vulnerable
pupils within the disciplinary constraints of secondary
education. Social workers, especially those who liaise with
schools, and educational psychologists will also need to

work out how best their contributions can be made to the families of teenagers at risk.

On the positive side, these figures show that most young people have a sense of purpose and find life worth living. Loneliness is no problem for the vast majority of young people and nearly a third do not feel depressed. This is the group which presents the conventional face of the young: happy, interested in life and sociable.

Males and females show a different pattern on depression, sense of purpose, self-worth and suicide. The females are more likely to have a sense of purpose in life and, at the same time, are more likely to be depressed, or to have a low self-image or to consider suicide. Thus it cannot be true to say that a sense of purpose lifts depression or relieves thoughts of suicide. Rather, people in general and females in particular, have a sense of purpose in spite of emotional unhappiness or low self-esteem.

Church attendance appears to give people a sense of purpose. Those who attend church weekly have a much greater sense of purpose than those who never attend, and this sense of purpose is reflected in the lower frequency of suicidal thoughts among churchgoers and their slightly greater sense of personal worth. On the other hand, church-goers suffer depressing thoughts as often as do non-attenders. Going to church therefore does not remove depression, but it does give a sense of purpose or reason for living. It is also associated with slightly lower levels of loneliness. More churchgoers find life worth living than do non-churchgoers. When it is considered that these figures are based on the responses of males and females in their mid-teens, the caricature of churchgoing as a boring ritual, alien to the young, may begin to be dispelled. On the contrary, the young people who attend church weekly have a greater sense of well-being than do non-attenders.

Although this conclusion may stand, it will need to be supplemented by further analysis and research since it is possible that the family situations of churchgoers are more stable, supportive or intimate. Moreover, teenage churchgoers tend to be female (in a ratio of two-thirds to one third). Nevertheless churchgoing clearly has a measurable effect on well-being since, even though girls are more likely to attend than boys, the percentage of church attenders with suicidal thoughts is lower than that for boys and girls separately (as comparing tables 4.2 and 4.4 shows).

Much of what may be said about churchgoers may also be said about those who believe in God without attending church. More non-churchgoing theists have a sense of purpose and a sense that life is worth living than do atheists. Believing in God appears to be beneficial to two important aspects of well-being, but it does not protect young people from depression.

So far as the denominations are concerned, the relatively high number of Anglican, Roman Catholic and Free Church young people who have considered suicide should be taken seriously by clergy. Most clergy would be unpleasantly surprised to discover that between a quarter and a fifth of their mid-teen young people had considered such a drastic course of action. There are obvious implications in these findings for clergy training, particularly for those who wish to specialise in a ministry to the young.

Reference

Woodroffe, C, Glickman, M, Barker, M and Power, C (1993), *Children, Teenagers and Health: the key data*. Buckingham, Open University Press.

5   My area

Introduction

This chapter examines young people's perceptions of the area where they live. Three statements concern positive features of the area: 'I like living in my area', 'I like my area as a shopping centre' and 'My area cares about its young people'. The remaining statements ask young people about behaviour associated with law-breaking or the disruption of social order: 'Vandalism is a growing problem in my area', 'Crime is a growing problem in my area', 'Violence is a growing problem in my area', 'Drunks are a growing problem in my area' and 'Drug taking is a growing problem in my area'. Finally, 'Unemployment is a growing problem in my area' deals with one possible cause of social decay.

Overview

Three-quarters (76%) of young people like living in their areas. Nearly half (47%) of young people like their local shopping facilities and a fifth (21%) think their area cares for the young. However, 13% of young people do not like their areas and nearly a third (31%) do not care for the local shops; a similar number (36%) says that its area does not care about its young people.

Table 5.1   My area: overview

	Agree %	Not certain %	Disagree %
I like living in my area	76	11	13
I like my area as a shopping centre	47	22	31
My area cares about its young people	21	43	36
Vandalism is a growing problem in my area	41	31	28
Crime is a growing problem in my area	36	35	29
Violence is a growing problem in my area	26	35	39
Unemployment is a growing problem in my area	31	47	22
Drug taking is a growing problem in my area	23	38	39
Drunks are a growing problem in my area	22	40	38

Vandalism and crime are thought to be on the increase by 41% and 36% respectively. Or, putting it the other way, less than a third of young people think vandalism (28%) or crime (29%) is not a growing problem locally. Similarly, there are rather more young people who see unemployment as a growing problem (31%) than do not (22%).

With regard to drugs, drunks and violence the figures are more optimistic. Fewer young people think these problems are growing than think they are not growing. Whereas 26% think that violence is growing, 39% think it is not; whereas 23% think drug taking is increasing, 39% think it is not; whereas 22% think there is a growing number of drunks, 38% think this is not so.

Does gender make a difference?

There is substantial agreement between the sexes about the areas where they live. Girls are slightly more fond than boys of their shopping facilities and boys slightly more positive than girls about other aspects of the locality. In their assessment of the area's problems there is substantial agreement about which are major and which are less serious. Vandalism, crime and unemployment are the top three problems and drunks, drugs and violence are the bottom three. Boys tend to be both more negative and more positive than girls; or, to put this another way, less undecided.

Table 5.2   My area: by gender

	Male %	Female %
I like living in my area	78	75
I like my area as a shopping centre	46	48
My area cares about its young people	23	19
Vandalism is a growing problem in my area	42	40
Crime is a growing problem in my area	39	33
Violence is a growing problem in my area	26	25
Unemployment is a growing problem in my area	30	32
Drug taking is a growing problem in my area	23	23
Drunks are a growing problem in my area	24	20

In detail the figures show that 46% of boys and 48% of girls like their area as a shopping centre, and that 32% of boys and 30% of girls do not like their area as a shopping centre. But the vast majority of both sexes (78% of boys and 75% of girls) have an overall liking for their areas, though 11% of boys and 14% of girls disagree. However, less than a quarter of boys (23%) and an even smaller number of girls (19%) think their area cares about its young people, and over a third of both sexes (38% of boys and 35% of girls) think their area has no care of young people.

While 42% of boys think vandalism is growing in their area, it is 40% of girls who agree with them; while 39% of boys think crime is growing locally, it is 33% of girls who agree with them; while 30% of boys think unemployment is growing locally, it is 32% of girls who agree with them; 23% of both sexes think that drug-taking is on the increase in their area; and, while 24% of boys think that drunks are a growing problem locally, it is 20% of girls who make the same assessment.

On the other hand, while 27% of boys do not think that unemployment is a growing problem locally, the same opinion is held by 18% of girls; 30% of boys and 27% of girls do not think that vandalism is increasing in their area; 31% of boys and 28% of girls do not think crime is increasing locally; two fifths (40%) of boys and 37% of girls do not think drunks are a growing problem in their area; 42% of boys and 36% of girls do not think that drugs are an increasing local problem and 43% of boys and 35% of girls consider that violence is not growing locally.

The uncertainty of girls on many of these issues is high. As many as half (50%) are not sure whether unemployment is rising and 46% cannot say whether their area cares about its young people. Over two fifths (43%) are not sure whether drunks are a growing problem. The percentage of uncertain boys on every item is between 5 and 9% lower than that of uncertain girls.

Does age make a difference?

The figures show that, as pupils move from year nine to year ten, they become less favourable to their area's amenities and, apart from unemployment, see their area's problems as being more serious. The sharpest increase occurs in the perception of drug-taking, crime, violence and vandalism. So, while 20% of year nine pupils see drug-taking as increasing, the figure a year later is 8% higher; while 34% of year nine pupils think crime is a growing problem, 5% more of year ten pupils make this judgement; while 24% of year nine pupils think violence is increasing, there is a 4% rise a year later in pupils who think the same thing; while 39% of year nine pupils see vandalism as a growing problem, a year later there is also a 4% increase in the number of pupils who come to this conclusion. Even the assessment of the problem of drunks goes up from 21% of pupils in year nine to 23% of pupils in year ten. Only with regard to unemployment does the percentage of year nine and year ten pupils remain the same (31%).

Table 5.3   My area: by age

	Year 9 %	Year 10 %
I like living in my area	79	73
I like my area as a shopping centre	48	46
My area cares about its young people	24	18
Vandalism is a growing problem in my area	39	43
Crime is a growing problem in my area	34	39
Violence is a growing problem in my area	24	28
Unemployment is a growing problem in my area	31	31
Drug taking is a growing problem in my area	20	28
Drunks are a growing problem in my area	21	23

The reverse perspective confirms these shifts in perception and judgement. While 42% of year nine pupils do not think drug taking is a growing problem, only 34% of year ten pupils take the same view; while 31% of year nine pupils do not think crime is a growing problem, it is only

28% of year ten pupils who agree; while 40% of year nine pupils do not think violence is increasing, this figure has dropped to 38% a year later; while 29% of year nine pupils think that vandalism is not on the increase, it is 28% of year ten pupils who agree with them; while 39% of year nine pupils do not think drunks are a growing problem, the percentage of year ten pupils who take this view is only 37%. Only unemployment is perceived differently. There is a slight rise in the percentage who think that it is not a growing problem (22% in year nine and 23% in year ten).

The appreciation of the local area as a shopping centre drops slightly from 48% of pupils in year nine to 46% of pupils in year ten, but more serious deterioration takes place in the numbers who think their area cares for its young people. There is a drop of 6% (from 24% in year nine to 18% in year ten) in the number of young people who think their area cares. There is a similar drop in the percentage of young people who like living in their area. This falls from 79% in year nine to 73% in year ten.

Again the reverse perspective confirms these findings. The percentage of those who dislike their area rises by 3% from 11% in year nine; similarly the percentage of those who dislike their area for shopping rises by 2% from 30% in year nine; and the percentage of those who think their area does not care for its young people rises by 7% from 33% in year nine.

Uncertainty levels remain similar, though on all issues (except if they like living in their areas) pupils are less uncertain as they get older.

Does church attendance make a difference?

This section examines pupils' perception of their area in the light of their church attendance and makes a comparison between three distinct groups: those who never attend church, those who attend sometimes and those who attend nearly every week.

The figures show that churchgoers perceive the growth or decrease of problems in their area very similarly to non-

churchgoers. Churchgoers, however, view the amenities of
their area more favourably than do non-churchgoers.

Table 5.4   My area: by church attendance

	Weekly %	Sometimes %	Never %
I like living in my area	80	77	74
I like my area as a shopping centre	48	47	47
My area cares about its young people	25	22	19
Vandalism is a growing problem in my area	39	41	41
Crime is a growing problem in my area	35	36	36
Violence is a growing problem in my area	26	25	26
Unemployment is a growing problem in my area	30	31	31
Drug taking is a growing problem in my area	21	23	24
Drunks are a growing problem in my area	23	22	22

Percentages of weekly, occasional or non-churchgoers do
not vary by more than 3% in their perception of the problems of vandalism, crime, violence, unemployment, drug
taking and drunks. On the reverse perspective there is a
slightly greater variation with regard to perceptions of
violence and drunks: whereas 35% of weekly churchgoers
think violence is not a growing problem, it is 39% of
occasional churchgoers and 40% of non-churchgoers who
take this view. There is a similar 5% difference between
weekly churchgoers and non-churchgoers in their perception
of drunks, and in both cases non-churchgoers are less
inclined to see any problem.

While 80% of weekly churchgoers like living in their
area, the corresponding figures for occasional churchgoers
and non-churchgoers are 77% and 74% respectively, and this
finding is confirmed by the reverse perspective. While 10%
of weekly churchgoers dislike living in their area, it is 12%
of occasional churchgoers and 14% of non-churchgoers who
take this view. In the same way 25% of weekly churchgoers
and 22% of occasional churchgoers think their area cares
about its young people, but slightly fewer non-churchgoers
(19%) feel this; the reverse perspective underlines this
finding by showing that, while 30% of weekly churchgoers

and 33% of occasional churchgoers do not think their area cares about its young people, it is 40% of non-churchgoers who feel similar neglect.

Does belief in God make a difference?

We now look at that subgroup of teenagers who never attend church, and explore the relationship between belief in God and ideas about the local area. The comparison is made between three groups of non-churchgoers: 'theists', 'agnostics' and 'atheists' (see page 7). Theists are more favourable in their assessment of the areas where they live than are agnostics, and agnostics are generally more favourable than atheists.

Table 5.5   *My area: by belief among non-churchgoers*

	Theist %	Agnostic %	Atheist %
I like living in my area	78	77	70
I like my area as a shopping centre	51	47	45
My area cares about its young people	22	19	19
Vandalism is a growing problem in my area	44	40	41
Crime is a growing problem in my area	40	33	36
Violence is a growing problem in my area	28	26	26
Unemployment is a growing problem in my area	34	31	30
Drug taking is a growing problem in my area	27	22	25
Drunks are a growing problem in my area	21	20	23

The figures show that 78% of theists, 77% of agnostics and 70% of atheists like their area; conversely 13% of theists, 12% of agnostics and 16% of atheists dislike living where they do. Over half of theists (51%) like the shopping facilities of their area, and this compares with 47% of agnostics and 45% of atheists; conversely 29% of theists do not like their shopping facilities, compared with 30% of agnostics and 34% of atheists. More than a fifth (22%) of theists think their area cares about its young people, whereas only 19% of agnostics and atheists agree; conversely 35% of theists, 36% of agnostics but 46% of atheists do not think their area cares for its young people.

When responses to social problems are compared, the findings are similar to those for the general population. Each of the three groups has more people in it who think vandalism, crime and unemployment are growing than think the opposite.

When the groups are compared with each other on these three main problems, more theists than agnostics and atheists think there is an increase locally. These findings are generally confirmed by the reverse perspective. It is 44% of theists, compared with 40% of agnostics and 41% of atheists, who think vandalism is a growing problem locally. The reverse perspective shows 26% of theists, 28% of agnostics and 32% of atheists think there is no growth in vandalism in the local area. Then, 40% of theists, 33% of agnostics and 36% of atheists think crime is a growing problem locally, whereas 28% of theists, 30% of agnostics and 33% of atheists reject this view. With regard to unemployment, 34% of theists, 31% of agnostics and 30% of atheists think the local figures are rising, but 21% of theists, 20% of agnostics and 26% of atheists disagree.

Problems associated with violence, drug taking and drunks are less likely to be seen by these three groups as rising in the local area. The figures show no clear pattern. While 28% of theists see violence as being on the increase in the local area, it is 26% of agnostics and atheists who take this view. The reverse perspective shows that 38% of theists and agnostics do not think violence is increasing locally, compared with 42% of atheists. Drug taking is thought to be on the increase by 27% of theists, 22% of agnostics and 25% of atheists, and the reverse perspective shows 39% of theists and 38% of the other two groups who disagree. Drunkenness is thought to be on the increase locally by 21% of theists, 20% of agnostics and 23% of atheists, whereas 41% of theists and atheists and 38% of agnostics disagree.

Does denomination make a difference?

The previous section looked at those who never attend church. This section examines those who attend church weekly, either in an Anglican, Free Church or Roman Catholic setting. The Free Church teenagers are fonder of their areas than are the Anglican or Roman Catholic teenagers and yet a higher percentage of Free Church teenagers perceive that vandalism, crime, violence, drug taking and problems with drunks are growing than is the case with the other churchgoing teenagers.

Table 5.6　My area: by denomination

	Catholic %	Anglican %	Free %
I like living in my area	79	81	83
I like my area as a shopping centre	47	47	50
My area cares about its young people	20	26	28
Vandalism is a growing problem in my area	35	42	43
Crime is a growing problem in my area	32	35	39
Violence is a growing problem in my area	25	24	26
Unemployment is a growing problem in my area	25	33	31
Drug taking is a growing problem in my area	19	16	24
Drunks are a growing problem in my area	19	21	27

While 83% of Free Church teenagers like living in their areas, it is 81% of Anglican and 79% of Roman Catholic teenagers who agree with them; while 50% of Free Church teenagers like their area for shopping, it is 47% of both Anglican and Roman Catholic teenagers who agree with them; while 28% of Free Church teenagers think their areas care about young people, it is 26% of Anglican and 20% of Roman Catholics who take this view.

The reverse perspective confirms two of these findings. Whereas 25% of Free Church young people do not think their area cares for its young, it is 29% of Anglican and 32% of Roman Catholic young people who take the same negative view. Similarly, 27% of Free Church, 28% of Anglican and 30% of Roman Catholic teenagers do not like their area for shopping. However, while 10% of both Free Church and Roman Catholic young people dislike their area, it is only 8% of Anglicans who do so.

The figures also show that, whereas 43% of Free Church and 42% of Anglican teenagers think that vandalism is a growing problem, it is 35% of Roman Catholic teenagers who think this is so. Whereas 39% of Free Church and 35% of Anglican teenagers think crime is a growing problem, it is 32% of Roman Catholic teenagers who think this is so. Whereas 27% of Free Church and 21% of Anglican teenagers think there is a growing problem with drunks, it is 19% of Roman Catholic teenagers who believe this to be the case. The reverse perspective shows even more marked differences. While 21% of Free Church and 24% of Anglican teenagers think that vandalism is not growing, it is 36% of Roman Catholic teenagers who hold this opinion; while 22% of Free Church and 26% of Anglican teenagers think that crime is not growing, it is 36% of Roman Catholic teenagers who take this view and, while 27% of Free Church and 35% of Anglican teenagers think that there is not a growing problem with drunks in their area, it is 40% of Roman Catholic teenagers who make this judgement.

Violence, unemployment and drug taking show a slightly different pattern. More Anglicans (33%) than Free Church teenagers (31%) or Roman Catholics (25%) think that unemployment is a growing problem in their area. More Free Church young people (24%) than Roman Catholic (19%) or Anglican (16%) young people see drug taking as a growing problem in their area. Percentages relating to violence do not vary by more than 2%: 26% of Free Church, 25% of Roman Catholic and 24% of Anglican young people see this as a growing problem in their area. The reverse perspective, however, shows that Free Church, Anglican and Roman Catholic young people, in that order, see these problems as on the increase. While 17% of Free Church and 21% of Anglican young people do not think unemployment is growing in their area, it is 24% of Roman Catholic young people who take this view; while 30% of Free Church and

34% of Anglican young people do not think violence is increasing in their area, it is 41% of Roman Catholic young people who think this to be the case; while 30% of Free Church and 39% of Anglican young people do not think that drug taking is a growing problem in their area, it is 44% of Roman Catholic young people who take this view.

Implications

These data show that three-quarters (76%) of young people like the area where they live. At the same time more young people think that vandalism, crime and unemployment are growing in their area than think the opposite. There are three main implications which could be drawn from this conjunction of figures: either the rise in crime and vandalism is so slow and gradual that it does not change the character of the area in which these young people live, or young people have simply adapted to crime and violence and learnt to accept it. Naturally there may also be some districts where vandalism, crime and unemployment are rising and others where they are not, and this may partially explain the figures. But *some* young people are living in areas which they like and which nevertheless are perceived to be suffering from growing social problems. This is evident because only 13% do not like the area where they live, but many more than this think that crime (36%) and vandalism (41%) are growing local problems.

Pupils in year ten more than in year nine see crime, vandalism and violence as on the increase in their area. This implies that year ten pupils are more aware of these problems than are year nine pupils, perhaps because crime, vandalism and violence are more likely to be committed by older pupils. A similar explanation makes sense when the figures on drug taking are examined. The figures for boys and girls are the same, but there is an upward jump of 8% between year nine and year ten. As pupils move up the school, they are more likely to take drugs or to have friends who take drugs. Their perception will then be that the problem is on the increase even though it may not be.

Churchgoers are not alarmist. Their perception of whether social problems are increasing is similar to that of the general population. Roman Catholic young people, however, are consistently *less* likely than the general population to see crime, vandalism, drugs, unemployment, drunks and violence as being on the increase in their area. This may simply be because the people with whom they mix are not involved in these social problems; alternatively, it may be that Roman Catholic teenagers were aware at a younger age than others of these problems and do not think there is any increase in them.

The twin findings that churchgoers like their area more than do non-churchgoers, and that Anglican and Free Church young people more than the general population think their area cares for its young, suggest either that churchgoers take a more positive view of their environment than others or that they live in more pleasant areas. Since churchgoers see social problems as clearly as non-churchgoers and since they are almost indistinguishable from non-churchgoers in their opinion of the shopping facilities of their area, it is likely that it is the network of relationships which churchgoers enjoy (partly or largely as a result of their churchgoing) which make them favour their areas more than do non-churchgoers. It is the personal relationships more than the physical environment which churchgoers like and which make their areas enjoyable.

This explanation fits young people's perception of the care offered by their area. While 30% of weekly churchgoers say their area does not care for its young, it is 40% of non-churchgoers who have the same complaint. Weekly churchgoers are more likely to be girls than boys, but more boys than girls (38% to 35%) think their area does not care for its young. Thus the lower number of weekly churchgoing young people who feel neglected by their areas must be connected with church attendance. If the church cares, young people are more likely to feel that the area cares. And, presumably, if young people feel that the area cares, they are less likely to indulge in vandalism and other anti-social behaviour.

Moreover it is difficult to establish a causal connection between unemployment and vandalism or crime by these figures alone. This is partly because those who seem most aware of vandalism and crime, that is, boys in year ten, are still at school and not yet subject to the job market; it is also because only a more sophisticated and wide-ranging statistical analysis making use of home, school and personality factors could disentangle the inter-correlations between possible causes of anti-social behaviour and various types of anti-social behaviour.

6 Concerns

Introduction

This chapter deals with the concerns of teenagers. Three statements approached the subject directly and began with the words, 'I am concerned about...'. The first statement referred to nuclear war, the second to poverty in the Third Word and the third to the risk of pollution to the environment. Two statements dealt with matters closer to home. 'There is too much violence on television' and 'Pornography is too readily available' invited young people to think about broadcasting and newsagents. Finally, the statement, 'There is nothing I can do to solve the world's problems' enabled young people to evaluate their own sense of power or powerlessness.

Overview

Pollution is top of the list of young people's concerns, and this is followed by nuclear war and poverty in the Third World. Two-thirds of young people (66%) are concerned about pollution and only 9% feel no concern on the matter. While slightly more young people are concerned about nuclear war (63%) than are concerned about Third World poverty (60%), the reverse perspective changes the order; only 15% are not concerned about nuclear war and only 13% are not concerned about Third World poverty.

On a local level, pornography is a matter of concern for 31% of young people, while only 18% feel the same way about violence on television. The reverse perspective shows that a third (33%) of teenagers are unconcerned about the availability of pornography and three out of five (60%) are unconcerned about television violence. Whatever the level of their concerns, however, a quarter of young people (25%) feel that there is nothing they can do anyway to solve the world's problems. This feeling of powerlessness is rejected by 44% who take the view that there *is* something they can do to help solve the world's problems.

Table 6.1   Concerns: overview

	Agree %	Not certain %	Disagree %
I am concerned about the risk of nuclear war	63	22	15
I am concerned about the poverty of the Third World	60	27	13
There is too much violence on television	18	22	60
There is nothing I can do to solve the world's problems	25	31	44
I am concerned about the risk of pollution to the environment	66	25	9
Pornography is too readily available	31	36	33

On two items more than 30% of the teenagers cannot make up their minds. There are 31% of teenagers who cannot say one way or the other if they can do anything to help solve the world's problems. The issue of pornography is even more difficult for teenagers to judge (though, as we shall see, boys and girls think very differently on this matter) since 36% cannot make up their minds. Otherwise, 22% are unsure about the risk of nuclear war and television violence, 25% about pollution and 27% about poverty in the Third World.

Does gender make a difference?

There are clear differences between males and females about their concerns. Girls are generally more concerned than are boys, especially over pornography, poverty in the Third World and television violence. While 38% of girls are concerned over the availability of pornography, it is only 24% of boys who share their concerns; while 65% of girls are concerned about Third World poverty, it is only 54% of boys who feel the same way; while 23% of girls think there is too much violence on television, only 14% of boys agree. All these differences are confirmed by the reverse perspective, sometimes emphatically so. Thus while nearly half of the boys (49%) do not think pornography is too readily available, a mere 17% of girls share this view; while only one girl in twelve (8%) is unconcerned about Third World poverty, it is more than twice as many boys (18%) who share this attitude; while nearly half of the girls (49%) are unconcerned about television violence, the comparable figure for boys is 70%.

Table 6.2   Concerns: by gender

	Male %	Female %
I am concerned about the risk of nuclear war	62	65
I am concerned about the poverty of the Third World	54	65
There is too much violence on television	14	23
There is nothing I can do to solve the world's problems	30	21
I am concerned about the risk of pollution to the environment	66	65
Pornography is too readily available	24	38

With regard to the risk of nuclear war and pollution, the differences are less marked. While 65% of girls are concerned about nuclear war, it is slightly fewer boys (62%) who share their feelings; conversely, while only 10% of girls are unconcerned about the risk of nuclear war, nearly double the number of boys (19%) take the same calm attitude. While 65% of girls are concerned about pollution to the environment, slightly more boys (66%) share their concerns; but the reverse perspective shows that girls have a more sensitive environmental conscience than do boys since, while 11% of boys are unconcerned about pollution, it is only 8% of girls who take this view.

With regard to their feelings of power or powerlessness, it is the girls more than the boys who feel they can make a contribution to solving the world's problems. While nearly a third of boys (30%) think they can do nothing to help, it is only 21% of girls who take this gloomy view; and this finding is confirmed by the percentages who feel that they can make a positive contribution. While 41% of boys feel there is something they can do for the world's problems, it is 46% of girls who share this view.

The uncertainty figures contain one surprise. A large number of girls, as many as 45%, is uncertain about the availability of pornography. The corresponding number of boys is 27%. Boys, in the main, can make up their minds on the issue, but girls are not so sure what to think.

Does age make a difference?

The age trend reveals that young people become less concerned as they pass from year nine to year ten. This is a consistent finding on all the topics covered in this survey except pornography. Concern about pornography has a pattern of its own which we discuss at the end of the chapter.

Table 6.3   Concerns: by age

	Year 9 %	Year 10 %
I am concerned about the risk of nuclear war	64	62
I am concerned about the poverty of the Third World	60	60
There is too much violence on television	19	17
There is nothing I can do to solve the world's problems	26	24
I am concerned about the risk of pollution to the environment	66	65
Pornography is too readily available	30	33

While 64% of year nine pupils are concerned about the risk of nuclear war, only 62% of year ten pupils are still concerned; while 19% of year nine pupils are concerned about television violence, this figure has dropped to 17% within the year; while 66% of pupils are concerned in year nine about pollution, it is 65% who continue to be concerned in year ten. The percentage of pupils concerned about

Third World poverty remains at 60% over the two years, but as we shall see the reverse perspective shows unconcern to increase. However, whereas 30% of year nine pupils are concerned about pornography, it is a larger number (33%) who are concerned a year later.

The reverse perspective finds that, while 14% of year nine pupils are unconcerned about nuclear war, it is 15% who feel this way a year later; while 58% of year nine pupils are unconcerned about too much television violence, it is 62% who agree with them in year ten; while 9% of pupils are unconcerned about pollution in year nine, it is 10% who are lacking in concern in year ten; while 12% of pupils are unconcerned about Third World poverty in year nine, it is 14% who feel this way a year later. With regard to pornography, while 32% of pupils in year nine express unconcern, the comparable figure in year ten is 33%.

Uncertainty figures vary by no more than 4% between year nine and year ten on any item.

Does church attendance make a difference?

This section examines pupils' concerns in the light of their church attendance and makes a comparison between three distinct groups: those who attend church weekly, those who attend church sometimes and those who attend church nearly every week. Churchgoers are consistently more concerned than non-churchgoers, and weekly churchgoers are consistently more concerned than occasional churchgoers. In addition, churchgoers are more likely to feel there is something they can do to help solve the world's problems.

The greatest disparity of concern occurs on the matter of Third World poverty. While over three-quarters (79%) of weekly churchgoers feel concerned, it is only 51% of non-churchgoers who agree. Conversely while only 6% of weekly churchgoers are unconcerned about Third World poverty, it is 17% of non-churchgoers who share this lack of concern.

A difference in concern on other topics is very apparent, but slightly less marked. Thus, while 69% of weekly churchgoers are concerned about the risk of nuclear war, it is only 59% of non-churchgoers who are concerned; while 27% of weekly churchgoers think there is too much violence on television, it is only 15% of non-churchgoers who think so; while 74% of weekly churchgoers are concerned about the risk of pollution to the environment, it is 59% of non-churchgoers who feel the same way; while 41% of weekly churchgoers are concerned about the availability of pornography, it is 28% of non-churchgoers who share this view.

Table 6.4   Concerns: by church attendance

	Weekly %	Sometimes %	Never %
I am concerned about the risk of nuclear war	69	68	59
I am concerned about the poverty of the Third World	79	67	51
There is too much violence on television	27	21	15
There is nothing I can do to solve the world's problems	15	21	30
I am concerned about the risk of pollution to the environment	74	73	59
Pornography is too readily available	41	33	28

The reverse perspective demonstrates the strength of these findings. While 10% of weekly churchgoers are unconcerned about the risk of nuclear war, it is 18% of non-churchgoers who share their equanimity; while 46% of weekly churchgoers are unconcerned about violence on television, it is two-thirds (66%) of non-churchgoers who hold the same attitude; while 8% of weekly churchgoers are unconcerned about the risk of pollution, it is 13% of non-churchgoers who are equally unconcerned; while 22% of weekly churchgoers have no concern about the availability of pornography, it is over a third (36%) of non-churchgoers who are similarly unconcerned.

The differences in levels of concern are accompanied by a greater sense among churchgoers that they can do something positive to help solve the world's problems. While 58% of weekly churchgoers feel this way, it is only 38% of non-churchgoers who feel that their contribution will count. Conversely, only 15% of churchgoers, as compared with twice as many (30%) non-churchgoers, feel that there is nothing they can do to help solve the world's problems.

These comparisons have been made between weekly churchgoers and non-churchgoers. In all five areas of concern the percentages of occasional churchgoers are consistently intermediate, on both the positive and negative perspectives, between these two main groups. They are also intermediate in their sense of power or powerlessness in the face of these problems.

Does belief in God make a difference?

We now look in detail at that subgroup of teenagers who do not go to church and we explore the relationship between belief in God and their levels of concern. The comparison is made between three groups of non-churchgoers: 'theists', 'agnostics' and 'atheists' (See page 7).

Table 6.5   Concerns: by belief among non-churchgoers

	Theist %	Agnostic %	Atheist %
I am concerned about the risk of nuclear war	67	60	52
I am concerned about the poverty of the Third World	60	53	43
There is too much violence on television	20	15	13
There is nothing I can do to solve the world's problems	28	26	35
I am concerned about the risk of pollution to the environment	66	60	55
Pornography is too readily available	32	29	25

Theists are more concerned than agnostics on every issue and agnostics are more concerned than atheists on every issue. These different levels of concern are generally confirmed by the reverse perspective. Theists and agnostics believe there is more they can do to solve the world's problems than do atheists.

The figures show that, whereas 60% of theists and 53% of agnostics are concerned about Third World poverty, it is only 43% of atheists who share this concern. Conversely, while 12% of theists and 11% of agnostics are unconcerned about Third World poverty, it is as many as 27% of atheists who profess to be without concern on this issue. Whereas 67% of theists and 60% of agnostics are concerned about the risk of nuclear war, it is only 52% of atheists who feel the same way. Conversely, 13% of both theists and agnostics are free of concern about the risk of nuclear war, compared with a quarter (25%) of atheists. Similarly, whereas 66% of theists and 60% of agnostics are concerned about pollution of the environment, only 55% of atheists share these concerns. From the reverse perspective, while only 9% of theists and agnostics do not care about the risk of pollution, it is twice as many atheists (18%) who are without concern in this matter.

Even the domestic issues show the same pattern. Thus, while 20% of theists and 15% of agnostics think there is too much television violence, it is a smaller number of atheists (13%) who share this concern; from the reverse perspective the figures show that, while 60% of theists and 63% of agnostics are unconcerned about small screen violence, it is nearly three-quarters of atheists (72%) who feel the same way. Pornography is a matter of concern for 32% of theists, 29% of agnostics and 25% of atheists or, to put this finding the other way, 31% of theists and agnostics do not think pornography is too readily available, compared with a significantly larger percentage of atheists (43%).

In looking at the perception which each of the three groups of teenagers has of its own power or powerlessness, it is the theists and agnostics who are most confident that they can make a difference. Two-fifths of theists (40%) and 39% of agnostics think there is something they can do about the world's problems, but the number of atheists who share this optimism is 35%; conversely, a quarter of agnostics (26%) and 28% of theists pessimistically feel there is nothing they can do about world problems, compared with a larger percentage of atheists (35%).

The uncertainty figures show that agnostics are consistently less sure than are theists or atheists. Indeed, on three issues more than a third of agnostics cannot make up their minds: poverty in the Third World (36%), whether they can help solve the world's problems (35%) and pornography (40%).

Does denomination make a difference?

The previous section looked at those who never attend church. This section examines those who attend weekly, either in an Anglican, Free Church or Roman Catholic setting.

Table 6.6   Concerns: by denomination

	Catholic %	Anglican %	Free %
I am concerned about the risk of nuclear war	72	70	68
I am concerned about the poverty of the Third World	83	80	84
There is too much violence on television	24	25	32
There is nothing I can do to solve the world's problems	16	15	11
I am concerned about the risk of pollution to the environment	73	75	77
Pornography is too readily available	41	38	43

Although the strength of feeling about the various issues varies between the different denominational groups, these young churchgoers agree on the order or priority of their concerns. The highest percentage in each denomination feels concerned about Third World poverty (80% of Anglicans, 83% of Roman Catholics and 84% of Free Church teenagers). The next highest percentage is concerned about pollution (75% of Anglicans, 73% of Roman Catholics and 77% of Free Church teenagers). Following this, the risk of nuclear war is on the minds of these young people (70% of

Anglicans, 72% of Roman Catholics and 68% of Free Church teenagers). Pornography ranks fourth on their list of concerns (38% of Anglicans, 41% of Roman Catholics and 43% of Free Church teenagers). Finally, the matter of least concern among the issues included in this survey is television violence (25% of Anglicans, 24% of Roman Catholics and 32% of Free Church teenagers).

This order of concerns is confirmed by the reverse perspective. Only a handful of churchgoing teenagers is unconcerned about Third World poverty (5% of Anglicans, 4% of Roman Catholics and 3% of Free Church people) and an only slightly larger number in each denomination is unconcerned about pollution (9% of Anglicans, 7% of Roman Catholics and 5% of Free Church people). The risk of nuclear war is a matter of indifference to a slightly larger number again (7% of Anglicans, 11% of Roman Catholics and 10% of Free Church people). Pornography is viewed with unconcern by 18% of both Anglican and Free Church young people and 28% of Roman Catholics; television violence is viewed with unconcern by the largest number in each group (44% of Anglicans, 54% of Roman Catholics and 32% of Free Church people).

The figures show that more Free Church young people (32%) tend to be concerned than Anglicans (25%) and Roman Catholics (24%) about television violence, but that otherwise the differences between these teenagers are small, no more than four percentage points.

With regard to the sense of a personal ability to solve the world's problems, the Free Church young people are more optimistic than are the Anglicans and the Roman Catholics. Over two-thirds (67%) of Free Church young people think that they can do something to make a difference to the world's problems, and this compares with 58% of Anglicans and 57% of Roman Catholics; conversely, only 11% of Free Church young people feel there is nothing they can do to solve the world's problems, compared with 15% of Anglicans and 16% of Roman Catholics.

The highest level of uncertainty is provoked by concern about pornography (44% of Anglicans, 31% of Roman Catholics and 39% of Free Church young people) and the lowest level of uncertainty affects concern about Third World poverty (15% of Anglicans and 13% of both Roman Catholic and Free Church young people). Otherwise uncertainty on the other issues varies by no more than five percentage points.

Implications

Pollution is the matter of greatest concern to this age group of young people. Green issues have come to the fore and these figures show that ecological and environmental matters have caught the attention of the next generation of voters. Nevertheless it is not possible to draw a simple equation between concerns and voting patterns since these young people give the risk of nuclear war and Third World poverty an almost equally high rating. There is little or no evidence that young people are campaigning for nuclear disarmament in the way that recalls the height of the Cold War, nor are they putting pressure on their parents or the government to increase British aid programmes overseas. Instead the behaviour of young people is reflected in a less intense way. They give to charitable appeals on television when famines strike and they adjust their buying habits to avoid ecologically insensitive producers. This analysis of the way these concerns are treated is supported by the fact that less than half (44%) of young people think that there is anything they can do to help solve the world's problems; in practice, this is not a campaigning cohort of young people. The suggestion that it is by using their purchasing power, rather than by marches and demonstrations, that these concerns will be expressed is made more likely by the greater sense that girls have that *they* can do something to help.

The ready availability of pornography is a concern for young people and not simply the preserve of campaigners like Mrs Whitehouse. It is girls, particularly, who are more likely to find pornography distasteful and boys who are more likely to find it acceptable. The 32% difference among those who think that pornography is *not* too readily available (boys 49%, girls 17%) is one of the largest divergencies between the sexes brought to light by this survey. Moreover, what table 6.3 shows is that concern about pornography increases between years nine and ten, and that this is the only issue on which concern increases. At the same time there is a slight increase in the percentage (32% in year nine and 33% in year ten) who do not think pornography is too readily available. There must be a polarisation of opinion over the year, and slightly more young people who were uncertain in year nine about pornography have decided against it than those who decided the other way.

Church attendance is associated with two things: a greater sense of concern on a wide range of issues and a greater sense of being able to make a positive contribution to world problems. The figures, for example, show that overall 60% of all young people in years nine and ten are concerned about Third World poverty, that 65% of girls are concerned, but that 79% of weekly churchgoers are concerned. Church-going is either a sensitising process or, through the teaching and preaching young people receive, it raises their awareness of human need and environmental danger. The relative similarity of the figures for Anglican, Roman Catholic and Free Church young people suggests that levels of concern are not raised by any one or obvious ecclesiastical factor.

Moreover, the change in priorities between churchgoers and the rest of the population is significant. While the general population places pollution as top of its list of concerns, churchgoers place poverty in the Third World as the top of their list. This change in the order of priorities is not made at the expense of a concern for the environment because the percentage of weekly and occasional church-goers who are concerned about the dangers of pollution is higher than that found in the population as a whole. Church-goers appear to have a real concern for fellow human beings; the humanitarianism of Christian young people is coupled with 'life stance' far more obviously than is the case with atheists.

From the point of view of the churches, the greater sense that churchgoers have than their contemporaries that they can help to solve world problems is encouraging. There must be a sense of latent activism in the pews and church youth clubs. While 38% of non-churchgoers think that they can make a difference to the world's problems, the comparable figure for weekly churchgoers is 58%. This suggests that the kind of faith these Christian young people espouse is not purely contemplative and academic, but practical and noticeable. To underline this point, a comparison between non-churchgoing atheists and churchgoers shows that it is the churchgoers (58%) who feel relatively effective in the face of the world's problems and the atheists (35%) who feel relatively powerless. Clergy, therefore, need to be ready to harness the energy and enthusiasms of young people and to understand the effects of the faith they preach. Christianity appears to give young people a sense of purpose and sense of empowerment. This in itself may be an attraction to many churchgoing teenagers.

Roman Catholic clergy, however, need to be aware that some of their young people are rather nearer to the opinions of the non-churchgoing population on the issues of pornography and television violence than is the case in other church groups. The figures show that in the percentage of those who are concerned about television violence and pornography, Roman Catholic young people are similar to Anglican and Free Church teenagers; but among those who do not care about these issues, there are 10% more of Roman Catholic young people than is the case in the other two denominational groups. This suggests that there is a fringe of young people attached to the Roman Catholic church whose opinions may be formed more by their secular peer group than by their church.

7   Sexual morality

Introduction

In this chapter we set out to profile the attitudes of teenagers to aspects of sexual morality. In order to sample the teenagers' views on human sexuality, six specific topics relating to sexual issues were incorporated within the survey. The six issues we selected were: sexual intercourse under the legal age of consent; sexual intercourse outside marriage; the use of contraception; abortion; divorce; and homosexuality. In our analysis of the data we were not only interested in the headline figures of how teenagers as a whole responded to each issue, but we were also concerned to discover how these views varied according to the ages, genders, and religious practice, belief and affiliation of the respondents.

Overview

It is clear from the survey results that the majority of 13 to 15 year olds do not use a set of moral absolutes to define their attitudes to human sexuality. Only a handful of young people (5%) feel that contraception is wrong. Only one in eight (13%) feel that it is wrong to have sexual intercourse outside marriage, and when it comes to the issue of whether it is wrong to have sexual intercourse under the legal age of consent, only one in four (24%) would agree that it is. Divorce is judged to be wrong by one in five (20%). The overwhelming message given by these figures is one of tolerance to most forms of sexual behaviour.

These generally 'liberal' beliefs can be contrasted with the somewhat more conservative positions young people in this age group take on the issues of abortion and homosexuality. Nonetheless, under two-fifths of them consider abortion (38%) or homosexuality (39%) to be wrong.

In the areas of sexual intercourse outside marriage, sexual intercourse under the legal age of consent, contraception and divorce, the balance of teenage opinion is clear. While 5%

feel that contraception is wrong, 72% confidently reject this view. Similarly, while 13% believe that it is wrong to have sexual intercourse outside marriage, 70% are clear that there is nothing wrong in such behaviour. Again, while 20% feel that divorce is wrong, over two and a half times this number (54%) think that divorce is morally acceptable. Finally, the one-quarter (24%) who think it is wrong to have sexual intercourse under the legal age of consent were outnumbered by more than two to one (54%) by those who took the opposite view.

Table 7.1   Sexual morality: overview

	Agree %	Not certain %	Disagree %
It is wrong to have sexual intercourse outside marriage	13	17	70
Divorce is wrong	20	26	54
Contraception is wrong	5	23	72
Abortion is wrong	38	30	32
It is wrong to have sexual intercourse under the legal age (16 years)	24	22	54
Homosexuality is wrong	39	25	36

On the other hand, as we have seen above, teenage opinion is more evenly divided on abortion and homosexuality. Compared with the 38% who consider abortion to be wrong, another sizeable percentage (32%) is convinced that it can be right. On homosexuality the numbers are even closer, where the 39% who consider it morally wrong are nearly matched (36%) by the number who are confident that it is right.

One further fact is evident from the data. Overall it is clear that a significant proportion of young people in this age group has still not formed definite opinions on the range of complex issues raised by human sexuality. Least uncertainty surrounds the issue of sexual intercourse outside marriage, but even here a sizeable minority (17%) does not know what to think. Around a quarter have no clear view on the morality of sexual intercourse under the legal age of consent (22%), contraception (23%), homosexuality (25%) and divorce (26%). On the morality of abortion the proportion of those who have not formed a clear view rises to 30%.

Having looked at the headline figures for these issues, we can now explore these questions in more detail using the criteria familiar from previous chapters.

Does gender make a difference?

The short answer to the question of gender differences in attitudes towards areas of human sexuality is, 'yes'. There are some important differences between male and female teenagers.

Table 7.2   *Sexual morality: by gender*

	Male %	Female %
It is wrong to have sexual intercourse outside marriage	13	13
Divorce is wrong	24	17
Contraception is wrong	8	3
Abortion is wrong	33	42
It is wrong to have sexual intercourse under the legal age (16 years)	18	29
Homosexuality is wrong	55	24

In some areas the boys adopt a more conservative moral framework than the girls. We find, for example, that the boys are twice as likely as the girls to regard homosexuality as morally wrong (55% against 24%). They are also twice as likely as the girls to regard contraception as wrong (8% against 3%). Similarly, 24% of the boys regard divorce as wrong, compared with 17% of the girls. To reverse our perspective, 48% of the girls argue that homosexuality is morally acceptable, compared with 24% of the boys. This pattern holds true for other issues also, although the figures do not contrast so sharply. On contraception 78% of the girls argue that it is morally acceptable, compared with 66%

of the boys, and on divorce 58% of the girls argue that it is morally acceptable, compared with 50% of the boys.

This differential does not hold good for all issues however. In some areas, particularly those which might be associated with childbirth, it is the girls who are more conservative than the boys. Thus, we find that 29% of the girls believe that it is wrong to have sexual intercourse under the legal age of consent, compared with 18% of the boys, and similarly 42% of the girls hold abortion to be wrong, against 33% of the boys. Looked at from another perspective, nearly two-thirds (62%) of the boys believe that it is morally acceptable to have sexual intercourse under the legal age of consent, compared with less than half (48%) of the girls. A third of the boys (32%) and a third of the girls (32%) believe that abortion is morally acceptable.

Given the above, it might seem that different systems of belief are being developed depending on a teenager's gender; we discuss the implications of this at the end of the chapter. However, although there are considerable areas of divergence in the attitudes of girls and boys, there are also many points of agreement. The same proportions of boys and girls (13%) agree that it is wrong to have sexual intercourse outside marriage and almost the same percentages (71% of the boys and 69% of the girls) find no moral objection to this sort of sexual activity.

Again roughly the same proportions of boys and girls are uncertain about their attitude towards sexual intercourse outside marriage (15% and 18%), sexual intercourse under the legal age of consent (21% and 23%), and divorce (26% and 25%).

Differences between the boys and the girls are also revealed by the percentages registering uncertainty. The boys are less likely to have made up their minds about issues like contraception (27% uncertain, compared with 19% of the girls) and abortion (34% uncertain, compared with 26% of the girls). On the other hand, the girls are less likely to have made up their minds on the issue of homosexuality, 29% being uncertain, compared with 21% of the boys.

Does age make a difference?

It is clear from the data that there is an overall progression of liberalisation in teenage sexual moral values between year nine and year ten. For example, 26% of year nine pupils argue that it is wrong to have sexual intercourse under the legal age of consent. By year ten the proportion has fallen to 20%. Again, while 41% of year nine pupils argue that abortion is wrong, the proportion falls to 34% among year ten pupils. In relation to sexual intercourse outside marriage the same pattern is repeated, with a drop from 15% for year nine pupils to 11% for year ten pupils. It is only in relation to homosexuality that this trend towards liberalisation does not occur so clearly.

Table 7.3   Sexual morality: by age

	Year 9 %	Year 10 %
It is wrong to have sexual intercourse outside marriage	15	11
Divorce is wrong	22	19
Contraception is wrong	6	4
Abortion is wrong	41	34
It is wrong to have sexual intercourse under the legal age (16 years)	26	20
Homosexuality is wrong	39	40

What the figures show is that there is a rise in the proportion of pupils who confidently reject moral absolutes in the context of sexual morality. This pattern emerges in relationship to issue after issue. While 65% of year nine pupils reject the view that contraception is wrong, by year ten the figure has risen to 80%. The 67% of year nine pupils who reject the view that it is wrong to have sexual intercourse outside marriage swell to 74% by year ten. The same pattern emerges for sexual intercourse under the legal age of consent (51% to 59%), divorce (52% to 56%) and abortion (29% to 36%). A more liberal position on homosexuality also emerges with a rise in those who find it morally acceptable (from 34% in year nine to 38% in year ten).

The other significant shift between year nine and year ten concerns a reduction in the proportion of pupils who register *uncertainty* in relation to issues of sexual morality. Over the range of the six questions concerned with aspects of sexual morality, an average of 25% of year nine pupils ticked the uncertain response category. By year ten this average has fallen slightly to 21%.

Does church attendance make a difference?

In order to answer this question we explore the attitudes towards sexual morality held by three distinct groups: those who never attend church, those who attend sometimes, and those who attend nearly every week. The statistics confirm that church attendance is a significant predictor of individual differences in adolescent attitudes towards sexual morality.

Table 7.4   Sexual morality: by church attendance

	Weekly %	Sometimes %	Never %
It is wrong to have sexual intercourse outside marriage	25	13	10
Divorce is wrong	27	20	19
Contraception is wrong	6	5	5
Abortion is wrong	50	36	35
It is wrong to have sexual intercourse under the legal age (16 years)	40	25	19
Homosexuality is wrong	37	35	43

There is a particularly clear trend in the relationship between church attendance and attitude towards sex outside marriage. Whilst 10% of those who never attend church believe that it is wrong to have sexual intercourse outside marriage, the proportion rises to 13% among those who attend church sometimes and 25% among those who attend church weekly. While 19% of those who never attend church believe that it is wrong to have sexual intercourse under the

legal age of consent, the proportions rise to 25% among
those who attend church sometimes and 40% among those
who attend church weekly. To look at these figures in
another light, the idea that it is wrong to have sexual intercourse outside marriage is denied by 76% of those who
never attend church, 69% of those who attend sometimes
and 50% of those who attend weekly. The idea that it is
wrong to have sexual intercourse under the legal age of
consent is denied by 61% of those who never attend church,
51% of those who attend sometimes and 37% of those who
attend weekly.

In relationship to some areas, however, there is little
difference between the attitudes of those who attend church
sometimes and those who never attend. The real cut-off
point on these issues comes between those who attend
church weekly, and those who do not. Thus, while 19% of
those who never attend church and 20% of those who sometimes attend church consider that divorce is wrong, the
proportion rises to 27% among weekly churchgoers. The
view that divorce is wrong is denied by 44% of weekly
churchgoers, as against 53% of those who attend church
sometimes and 56% of those who never attend church.
While 35% of those who never attend church and 36% of
those who sometimes attend church consider abortion is
wrong, the proportion rises to 50% among weekly churchgoers. The view that abortion is wrong is denied by 20% of
weekly churchgoers, compared with 32% of those who
attend church sometimes and 35% of those who never attend
church.

Views on the morality of contraception are not significantly related to church attendance.

Teenagers who attend church weekly or less frequently
hold a more liberal attitude towards homosexuality than do
teenagers who do not attend church. The figures suggest that
37% of weekly churchgoers and 35% of occasional churchgoers regard homosexuality as wrong, compared with 43%
of non-churchgoers. This finding needs to be interpreted
with caution, however, since as we saw in a previous section

girls record a more liberal attitude towards homosexuality than do boys, and girls are more likely than boys to be churchgoers on an occasional or regular basis. It follows, therefore, that the apparent relationship between church attendance and a more liberal attitude to homosexuality may well be partly a result of differences in the attitudes of the sexes.

One other significant feature of the relationship between church attendance and teenage attitudes toward sexual morality deserves further comment. Overall, young church-goers are *less* likely to be certain about their views on aspects of sexual morality than young people who never attend church. Over the range of six questions concerned with aspects of sexual morality, an average of 27% of those who attend church weekly gave an uncertain response, compared with 23% of those who never attend church. This phenomenon is seen most starkly in the context of sex outside marriage. While 14% of those who never attend church remain uncertain about their view on the morality of sexual intercourse outside marriage, the proportion rises to 18% among occasional attenders and 25% among weekly attenders.

Does belief in God make a difference?

Having looked at the relationship between sexual morality and church attendance, we now move on to examine the influence of belief in God on the moral views of those who never attend church. In exploring the relationship between belief in God and attitudes towards sexual morality among those who do not attend church, our comparison is once more between 'theists', 'agnostics' and 'atheists' (see page 7). The statistics confirm that belief in God is a significant predictor of individual differences in adolescent attitudes towards sexual morality among those who have no direct contact with churches.

Among non-churchgoers, the clearest trend in the relation-ship between belief in God and an aspect of sexual morality, concerns the issue of sex outside marriage. Thus, 15% of the theists believe that it is wrong to have sexual intercourse outside marriage, compared with 10% of the agnostics and 9% of the atheists. This pattern is repeated elsewhere. While 25% of the theists believe that it is wrong to have sexual intercourse under the legal age of consent, only 20% of the agnostics and 15% of the atheists hold this similar view. Looked at from another point of view, the idea that it is wrong to have sexual intercourse outside marriage is clearly denied by 80% of the atheists, 74% of the agnostics and 70% of the theists. The idea that it is wrong to have sexual intercourse under the legal age of consent is denied by 69% of the atheists, 55% of the agnostics and 54% of the theists.

Table 7.5   Sexual morality: by belief among non-churchgoers

	Theist %	Agnostic %	Atheist %
It is wrong to have sexual intercourse outside marriage	15	10	9
Divorce is wrong	22	17	18
Contraception is wrong	7	4	6
Abortion is wrong	43	34	32
It is wrong to have sexual intercourse under the legal age (16 years)	25	20	15
Homosexuality is wrong	44	40	44

Belief in God also appears to have a significant impact on the attitudes of adolescents towards abortion and divorce. We find, therefore, that while 43% of the theists are clear that abortion is wrong, only 34% of the agnostics and 32% of the atheists would agree. Looked at from the reverse perspective, while 42% of atheists hold that abortion is not wrong, the proportion falls to 31% among the theists. Similarly, 22% of the theists are convinced that divorce is wrong, compared with 17% of the agnostics and 18% of the atheists.

However, once again this pattern does not hold good for all issues. Views on the morality of contraception and homosexuality do not seem to be significantly related to belief in God. Thus, 7% of the theists and 6% of the atheists believe that contraception is wrong, while 70% of theists and 73% of atheists deny this. At the same time, an equal percentage (44%) of theists and atheists are opposed to homosexuality, and almost an equal number of both groups believe that it is morally acceptable.

One other significant feature regarding the relationship between belief in God and teenage attitudes towards sexual morality also emerges from the data. There is a clear relationship between religious agnosticism and greater uncertainty about the acceptance or rejection of moral absolutes in sexual behaviour. Over the range of the six questions concerned with aspects of sexual morality, an average of 26% of agnostics checked the uncertain response, compared with 21% of the theists and 20% of the atheists. This phenomenon is seen most distinctly in relation to the issues of abortion and homosexuality.

While 26% of both the theists and the atheists remain uncertain about the morality of abortion, this proportion rises to 35% among the agnostics. On homosexuality, the comparison is between 21% of theists and 20% of atheists on the one hand and 28% of the agnostics on the other. It would appear, therefore, that those who are uncertain about the existence of God are uncertain about moral issues also.

Does denomination make a difference?

The previous section took a close look at the young people who never attend church. Now we take a close look at those who attend church weekly and explore the relationship between their denominational identity and their attitudes toward sexual morality.

The comparison here is between members of the Roman Catholic, Anglican and Free Churches. The statistics confirm the continued influence of clear emphases within denominational teaching on some aspects of sexual morality, as well as the clear rejection of other distinctive denominational emphases among teenage churchgoers. This dichotomy is clearly demonstrated by the contrasting views of Catholic teenagers to the issues of abortion and contraception.

Table 7.6   Sexual morality: by denomination

	Catholic %	Anglican %	Free %
It is wrong to have sexual intercourse outside marriage	22	22	30
Divorce is wrong	30	24	27
Contraception is wrong	5	4	8
Abortion is wrong	66	38	47
It is wrong to have sexual intercourse under the legal age (16 years)	32	41	47
Homosexuality is wrong	35	30	38

Teenage churchgoing Catholics are much more likely to espouse a more conservative view on the morality of abortion than are teenage churchgoers from Anglican or Free Church backgrounds. Thus, 66% of the churchgoing Catholics believe that abortion is wrong, compared with only 47% of those who attend Free Churches and 38% of young Anglicans. Again only 13% of churchgoing Catholics deny that abortion is wrong, compared with 19% of those who attend Free Churches and 27% of young Anglicans.

Contrary to the above example, teenage churchgoing Catholics' views on *contraception* are quite close to their contemporaries from other traditions. Thus, only 5% of Catholic teenagers believe that contraception is wrong, compared with 4% of Anglicans, and a slightly higher percentage (8%) of Free Church young people. Nearly three-quarters (72%) of churchgoing Catholic teenagers deny that contraception is wrong, compared with an identical number of Anglicans, and 65% of Free Church adherents.

Teenage churchgoers who attend one of the Free Churches are more likely than teenage churchgoing Catholics or Anglicans to espouse a conservative view on the morality of sex outside marriage. Almost one-third (30%) of those who attend one of the Free Churches believe that it is wrong to have sexual intercourse outside marriage, compared with less than a quarter of Anglicans and Catholics (22% in each case). Similarly, 47% of those who attend one of the Free Churches believe that it is wrong to have sexual intercourse under the legal age of consent, compared with 41% of Anglicans and 32% of Catholics.

In areas like homosexuality, divorce and abortion, teenage churchgoing Anglicans are likely to espouse a more liberal view than either of the other groups. Thus, 30% of Anglicans consider homosexuality wrong, compared with 35% of Catholic and 38% of Free Church members. Similarly, 24% of Anglicans believe divorce to be wrong, compared with 30% of Catholic and 27% of Free Church teenagers, and 38% of Anglicans are against abortion, compared with 66% of Catholic and 47% of Free Church teenagers.

Overall, young churchgoing Anglicans are less likely than the others to be certain about their views on the selected aspects of sexual morality. Over the range of six questions, an average of nearly 30% of Anglicans register their uncertainty, compared with 27% of Free Church teenagers and 24% of Catholics. This phenomenon is seen most starkly in relation to sex outside marriage, where a 30% uncertainty figure for churchgoing Anglicans compares with 24% for Catholics and 21% for Free Church adherents.

Implications

What clearly emerges from the totality of responses in this chapter is that the overwhelming majority of British teenagers hold liberal views on issues of sexual morality. Even if some degree of caution regarding sexual behaviour has been engendered by AIDS and AIDS advertising, the teenagers have not allowed such publicity to alter their general views on what is right and wrong. It would be fair to sum up by saying that sex is certainly on the agenda of these young people. The vast majority of those surveyed do not object to sex outside marriage. Moreover, the age trend suggests that those who do object will diminish to a comparatively small group as young people climb into their high teens.

To put this general liberal position into perspective, it is the case that on no issue is there a majority of teenagers who are prepared to apply moral blame to a particular sexual behaviour and its consequences. At no point do the majority of teenagers condemn a particular behaviour as wrong. Abortion and divorce are not given unqualified approval, but the majority of teenagers consider them to be unworthy of blame. Even under-age sex is by and large accepted.

On the positive side the very liberality of these attitudes would tend to imply that young people are prepared to live tolerantly and without guilt. The children of divorcees need not expect to be ostracised by their contemporaries, and they themselves may avoid feelings of guilt and rejection.

The only exception to this picture would appear to be in relation to homosexuality. The figures given here show that this practice is the most highly condemned of all and the age trend shows the graph of condemnation to be slanted upward. Teenage male homosexuals are likely to conform to the expectations of their age group to avoid trouble, but given the generally tolerant shape of the figures as a whole, greater tolerance of homosexuality is likely to emerge in the late teens and early twenties.

Positively, as we have said, these figures imply a great degree of tolerance among young people. When we turn to the negative consequences the picture changes. The new tolerance has been bought at the price of a virtual abandonment of traditional family values. If these young people gain the sexual experience for which most of them are looking, the majority of those who still come for a church wedding will have had sexual experience prior to marriage. The later they marry, the more likely this sexual experience will involve multiple partners. The churches which give pre-marital pastoral counselling will need to take such factors into account. Furthermore, there are statistics which suggest that those who have cohabited before marriage are actually *less* likely to realise a permanent marital relationship than those who have not. If these statistics are reliable, then the divorce rates of the last two decades are unlikely to turn down.

It may well be that the traditional family will increasingly become a social minority, as fewer and fewer people are prepared to accept the underlying assumptions on which it is based. Moreover, the combination of the figures on contraception and sexual intercourse outside marriage reveals a large number of young girls in danger of unwanted pregnancy. The girls who are uncertain about the rightness of sex outside marriage and uncertain about the rightness of contraception could find themselves pregnant if sexual opportunity presents itself. Since the number of girls who think that sex outside marriage is right is higher by 37% than the number who think that abortion is right, this group of girls may find themselves agonizing over doing what they believe to be wrong to extricate themselves from unwanted motherhood.

The large number of uncertain responses which pupils give to many of these moral issues suggests that there is a crucial role for moral education. Moral education does not necessarily bring with it moral certainty, but it should help to clarify moral issues. In the figures cited in this chapter there are typically one-fifth of pupils who are uncertain, and because the age trends show that there are changes in the agreement and disagreement responses, it is clear that pupils are changing their minds in the mid-teen years. This fluidity of opinion implies that pupils will be willing to discuss moral topics.

The differences in opinion between boys and girls demonstrate that objections to homosexuality are felt much more strongly by males. The dominant male teenage subculture stresses style, clothes, music and romantic love. It has comparatively little room for alternative sexuality. In any event it is unlikely that teenage male homosexuals will be sure whether their orientation is temporary or permanent. Even those who will eventually become adult male homosexuals may at this stage of their lives reject homosexuality. The reason for greater male rejection of homosexuality may be connected with the development of male identity after puberty.

The differences in opinion between boys and girls over contraception and under-age sex imply a female fear of unwanted pregnancy. It is difficult to see what moral principle is being invoked by largely non-Catholic males to condemn contraception or to hesitate in its use. More than a quarter of males are not sure whether contraception is right or wrong. The broader implications of these findings is that moral education or sex education are necessary to help pupils make up their minds. Certainly the fact that there is a conflict in the views of males and females over the use of contraception, and at the same time a broad acceptance of under-age sex, again puts the danger of teenage pregnancy into the spotlight.

Turning to church attendance and to the role of the churches in informing moral attitudes, the figures imply the generally liberal views of young churchgoers. Though this is something they share with non-churchgoers, it is still true that churchgoing young people have a stricter view of sexual morality than do their non-churchgoing peers. The differences are not overwhelming however, and are not great enough to overcome the general pattern.

Where young churchgoers take a different stance from the majority is in their greater unwillingness to express a firm opinion on issues of sexual morality. The larger number of uncertain responses among churchgoers may be interpreted as a consequence of conflict between two codes of moral behaviour: the church code which says that sex before marriage is wrong, and the prevailing youth culture which says that it is right. Teenage churchgoers caught in this conflict respond by leaving their moral decisions in the pending tray.

How should the churches respond to these findings? Clearly there are two possible approaches which they could adopt. First, they may wish to strengthen their moral teaching to young people in line with conventional Christian norms. Second, they may reject this approach and concentrate on helping young people to come to terms with the competing moral pressures to which they are subject. This may involve intellectual support as well as the social support offered by youth events like camps, retreats and seminars.

An examination of the figures presented in this chapter reveals that non-churchgoing theists are distinguishable from non-churchgoing atheists and agnostics. Two implications can be deduced from this finding. First, the young non-churchgoing theists are morally closer to the church and many share values in common with churchgoers. Second, belief in God does seem to function as a practical moral starting point. Belief in God makes a difference to the standards young people adopt on sexual morality, even without the social support given to moral values by direct contact with the churches.

Turning to the denominational figures, it would appear that the Roman Catholic church is not having the same success with its teaching on contraception as it enjoys with its teaching about abortion. There is an evident Catholic stance against abortion that is clearly reflected in the views held by their young people. At the same time, the well-known anti-birth control views of the Roman Catholic hierarchy do not find an echo among the views held by young Catholics.

Overall the figures even suggest that the young members of the Free Churches take a stronger line against contraception than do the young Catholics. This finding draws attention to a clear area of conflict which is likely to impinge on the lives of young Catholics at the time when they become sexually active. Moreover, direct confrontation with their church's teaching in this area may encourage young Catholics to challenge their church's teaching in other areas and may also precipitate lapsation from active membership and practice.

8   Right and wrong

Introduction

In this chapter we consider the moral code of young people. To sample this code we put forward eight statements. The first statement simply asserts, 'The police do a good job' and young people were invited to respond by registering agreement, disagreement or uncertainty. The remaining statements all started with the words, 'There is nothing wrong in...' and ranged over shop-lifting, travelling without a ticket, cycling after dark without lights, playing truant, buying cigarettes under the legal age, buying alcoholic drinks under the legal age and writing graffiti wherever you like.

Overview

Nearly two out of three young people (62%) agree that the police do a good job, but a fifth (20%) are not sure about this and almost the same number (18%) definitely think the police do not do a good job. The extent to which this criticism is related to ineffectiveness against crime or is simply an expression of anti-police sentiment is discussed at the end of this chapter.

Table 8.1   Right and wrong: overview

	Agree %	Not certain %	Disagree %
There is nothing wrong in:			
shop-lifting	7	8	85
travelling without a ticket	19	24	57
cycling after dark without lights	15	10	75
playing truant from school	18	19	63
buying cigarettes under the legal age (16 years)	27	16	57
buying alcoholic drinks under the legal age (18 years)	39	20	41
writing graffiti wherever you like	16	19	65
The police do a good job	62	20	18

On all the other moral matters sampled young people's opinions are stated remarkably consistently. Opinions about shop-lifting are very clear. The vast majority of young people (85%) thinks shop-lifting is wrong and only a small number (8%) is not certain and an even smaller number (7%) thinks that it is all right. The next most wrong activity is cycling after dark without lights. Three-quarters (75%) of young people consider that it is wrong to break the Highway Code in this way, and only 15% disagree. Ten percent are uncertain. Graffiti writing is viewed slightly more liberally (65% think that is wrong and 16% think it is acceptable) and playing truant is viewed more liberally still (63% think that it is wrong and 18% that it is all right). Travelling without a ticket is unacceptable to over half (57%), though nearly one in five (19%) disagree. Buying cigarettes under the legal age is also unacceptable to the majority (57%) of teenagers, though over a quarter (27%) consider it all right. Buying alcoholic drinks under the legal age is viewed most liberally of all. Nearly two out of every five young people (39%) think that it is morally right to break the law in this way and, while an almost equal number disagrees (41%), the remaining fifth (20%) are unable to make up their mind.

Does gender make a difference?

In general boys are more inclined to consider it acceptable to break rules than are girls. Boys are also more inclined to evaluate the police negatively. Whereas 14% of girls think the police are doing a bad job, the figure for boys is 23%. From the reverse perspective, whereas 64% of girls think the police do a good job, only 59% of boys agree.

In most of the other areas the greater willingness of boys to take risks by breaking moral rules stands out emphatically. Whereas 24% of boys think there is nothing wrong in riding a bicycle without lights in the dark, only 7% of girls agree with their view. In the same way, while less than two out of three boys (64%) think it *is* wrong to ride without lights, the figure for girls rises steeply to over four out of five (85%). Travelling without a ticket shows a similar pattern. As many as a quarter (25%) of boys have no problem doing this, but the figure for girls is only 13%. Turning the perspective round, the figures show 61% of girls think there is something wrong in this behaviour, compared with 53% of boys.

Table 8.2   Right and wrong: by gender

	Male %	Female %
There is nothing wrong in:		
shop-lifting	9	5
travelling without a ticket	25	13
cycling after dark without lights	24	7
playing truant from school	20	16
buying cigarettes under the legal age (16 years)	26	27
buying alcoholic drinks under the legal age (18 years)	42	36
writing graffiti wherever you like	19	13
The police do a good job	59	64

In their attitudes to shop-lifting, writing graffiti, truancy and buying alcohol under age, boys and girls are fairly close together, though the boys consistently adopt a more liberal moral code. While 5% of girls think shop-lifting is acceptable, the figure for boys is 9%; while 13% of girls think that writing graffiti is all right, the figure for boys is 19%; while 16% of girls condone truancy, it is 20% of boys who do so; while 36% of girls agree there is nothing wrong in buying alcohol under the legal age, 47% of boys take this view.

The glaring exception to this trend occurs with buying cigarettes under the legal age. Slightly *more* girls (27%) than boys (26%) think there is nothing wrong with buying cigarettes in this way and fewer girls (55%) than boys (60%) think there *is* something wrong in buying cigarettes under the legal age.

Does age make a difference?

Young people become more liberal, or less inclined to accept legal restrictions, as they pass through their mid-teens. They also become more critical of the police. Moreover, there is a slight shift (of no more than 2% on any item) towards increased uncertainty.

Table 8.3   Right and wrong: by age

	Year 9 %	Year 10 %
There is nothing wrong in:		
shop-lifting	7	7
travelling without a ticket	17	21
cycling after dark without lights	14	17
playing truant from school	16	20
buying cigarettes under the legal age (16 years)	22	32
buying alcoholic drinks under the legal age (18 years)	33	45
writing graffiti wherever you like	15	16
The police do a good job	64	59

The issue of buying alcohol under the legal age illustrates the main trend. While 33% of year nine pupils think there is nothing wrong with buying alcoholic drinks under the legal age, the figure for year ten pupils jumps to 45%. At the same time uncertainty increases from 20% to 21% over the two years and the number of teenagers who uphold the legal restriction on buying alcohol under the age of sixteen years drops from 47% to 34%. This pattern is repeated with under age buying of cigarettes (when 22% of year nine pupils think it acceptable compared with 32% of year ten pupils). Likewise there is a drop in those who support the legal restriction on cigarette buying under the legal age of sixteen years when the perspective is reversed (63% in year nine reduces to 51% in year ten).

On the other items the shift is in the same direction but less marked. Whereas 17% of year nine pupils think that there is nothing wrong in travelling without a ticket, the

figure for year ten pupils is 21%. In each case the shift is
between 1% and 4%. From the reverse perspective the shift
on each item is between 2% and 6%.

The item referring to the police indicates a drift to disaffection. While 64% of year nine pupils think the police do
a good job, only 59% of year ten pupils agree; whereas 16%
of year nine pupils definitely do not think the police do a
good job, by year ten this figure has risen to one in five
(20%).

Does church attendance make a difference?

The survey demonstrates unmistakably that churchgoing
pupils are more inclined to agree with keeping the law than
are non-churchgoing pupils. Churchgoers are also distinctly
more likely than non-churchgoers to accept that the police
are doing a good job.

Table 8.4   Right and wrong: by church attendance

	Weekly %	Sometimes %	Never %
There is nothing wrong in:			
shop-lifting	3	5	9
travelling without a ticket	11	15	23
cycling after dark without lights	8	11	20
playing truant from school	10	14	22
buying cigarettes under the legal age (16 years)	16	23	31
buying alcoholic drinks under the legal age (18 years)	27	35	44
writing graffiti wherever you like	10	13	19
The police do a good job	70	66	57

The figures are very consistent and clear. Whereas 27%
of weekly churchgoers think there is nothing wrong in
buying alcoholic drinks under age, the figure for non-
churchgoers is 44%; whereas 16% of weekly churchgoers
think there is nothing wrong in buying cigarettes under age,
for non-churchgoers the figure is 31%; whereas 10% of
weekly churchgoers think there is nothing wrong in playing

truant, for non-churchgoers the figure is 22%; whereas 11% of weekly churchgoers think there is nothing wrong in travelling without a ticket, for non-churchgoers the figure is 23%; whereas 8% of weekly churchgoers think there is nothing wrong in cycling after dark without lights, the figure for non-churchgoers is 20%; whereas 10% of weekly churchgoers think there is nothing wrong in writing graffiti anywhere, the figure for non-churchgoers is 19%. Only in the matter of shop-lifting is the percentage difference below double figures. Whereas 3% of weekly churchgoers think there is nothing wrong in shop-lifting, the figure for non-churchgoers is 9%.

The reverse perspective confirms all these findings. Weekly churchgoers consistently uphold the rightness of the moral behaviours sampled here. The gap between weekly churchgoers and non-churchgoers is between 16 and 19%, except with regard to shop-lifting when it drops to 10%.

Weekly churchgoers are more positive about the police than are non-churchgoers. Whereas 70% of weekly church-goers think the police do a good job, the figure for non-churchgoers is only 57%. In the same way 10% of weekly churchgoers do not agree that the police do a good job, as compared with 23% of non-churchgoers.

So far as uncertainty about right and wrong is concerned, weekly churchgoers are consistently more certain than non-churchgoers. For example, whereas 25% of non-churchgoers are uncertain about whether it is right or wrong to travel without a ticket, the figure for weekly churchgoers is 18%. The differences vary between 1% and 10%.

In all these figures (except one) occasional church attenders fall in an intermediate position between weekly churchgoers and non-churchgoers. The only exception in the whole table of figures concerns the uncertainty figure about buying alcohol under the legal age: whereas 20% of non-churchgoers are uncertain about such purchases, the figure for occasional church attenders is 21%.

Does belief in God make a difference?

We now turn to the analysis on those who do not go to church and make our usual comparison between three groups: 'theists', 'agnostics' and 'atheists' (see page 7). The statistics show that theists are more likely to have clear ideas of right and wrong and to accept a more strict moral code than are either of the other two groups. Or, to put this another way, atheists are more likely to consider there is nothing wrong with illegal behaviour and to be critical of the police.

Table 8.5   Right and wrong: by belief among non-churchgoers

	Theist %	Agnostic %	Atheist %
There is nothing wrong in:			
shop-lifting	6	7	13
travelling without a ticket	20	19	29
cycling after dark without lights	15	16	25
playing truant from school	18	19	27
buying cigarettes under the legal age (16 years)	27	28	36
buying alcoholic drinks under the legal age (18 years)	38	40	50
writing graffiti wherever you like	16	15	24
The police do a good job	64	60	51

While 6% of theists think there is nothing wrong in shop-lifting, more than twice as many atheists (13%) hold this opinion. Similarly, 20% of theists, compared with 29% of atheists, think there is nothing wrong in travelling without a ticket; 15% of theists, compared with 25% of atheists, think there is nothing wrong with cycling after dark without lights; 18% of theists, compared with 27% of atheists, think there is nothing wrong with playing truant; 27% of theists, compared with 36% of atheists, think there is nothing wrong in buying cigarettes under the legal age; 38% of theists, compared with 50% of atheists, think there is nothing wrong in buying alcohol below 16 years of age and 16% of theists, as compared with 24% of atheists, think there is nothing wrong in writing graffiti anywhere they like.

When the figures are examined to see what percentage of each group considers the various behaviours wrong, the theists consistently outnumber the atheists. So, whereas 88% of theists consider shop-lifting is wrong, only 77% of atheists do so. For each of the moral items the pattern is repeated and the difference between theists and atheists averages ten percentage points.

The statistics relating to the members of each group who register uncertainty show that the theists are, in most cases, more sure of their opinions than are atheists. The two exceptions concern buying cigarettes and alcoholic drinks under the legal age. So, for example, whereas 20% of theists are uncertain about buying alcohol, the figure for uncertain atheists only reaches 18%. In the other areas the percentage of uncertain theists is about 3% lower than for uncertain atheists. For instance 17% of theists are uncertain about truancy, as compared with 20% of atheists.

Theists are more likely to approve of the police (66%) than are atheists (51%). Only 18% of theists are critical of the police, as against 29% of atheists.

Agnostics in general fall between theists and atheists in their moral opinions. Thus, 60% of agnostics think that the police do a good job. On five of the items (travelling without a ticket, buying alcohol and cigarettes under the legal age, writing graffiti and the police) agnostics are more uncertain than the other two groups and on the others (shop-lifting and cycling) they are intermediate.

Does denomination make a difference?

Having looked in the previous section at the young people who never attend church, we turn to those who attend weekly. We explore the relationship between denominational identity and moral code, by comparing members of the Roman Catholic, Anglican and Free Churches.

The figures show that Anglican and Free Church young people stand close together and slightly apart from the

Roman Catholic young people. In each instance the Roman Catholics are more inclined than the other two groups to condone illegal behaviour and to be critical of the police. The differences are not great, but they are consistent.

Table 8.6   *Right and wrong: by denomination*

	Catholic %	Anglican %	Free %
There is nothing wrong:			
in shop-lifting	3	2	2
travelling without a ticket	13	8	9
cycling after dark without lights	11	6	5
playing truant from school	12	7	7
buying cigarettes under the legal age (16 years)	22	12	14
buying alcoholic drinks under the legal age (18 years)	32	24	22
writing graffiti wherever you like	13	7	7
The police do a good job	63	74	78

Thus, whereas 2% of Anglican and Free Church young people think that shop-lifting is wrong, 3% of Roman Catholic young people do so; whereas 8% of Anglican and 9% of Free Church young people think there is nothing wrong in travelling without a ticket, the figure for Roman Catholics is 13%; whereas 6% of Anglican and 5% of Free Church young people think there is nothing wrong in cycling without lights, the figure for Roman Catholics is 11%; whereas 7% of Anglican and Free Church young people think there is nothing wrong in playing truant, 12% of Roman Catholic young people think this; whereas 12% of Anglican and 14% of Free Church young people think there is nothing wrong in buying cigarettes under the legal age, the figure for Roman Catholic young people is 22%; whereas 24% of Anglican and 22% of Free Church young people think there is nothing wrong in buying alcoholic drinks under the legal age, it is 32% of Roman Catholics who take this view; whereas 7% of Anglican and Free Church young people think there is nothing wrong in writing graffiti, the figure for Roman Catholics is 13%. Similarly, whereas 74% of Anglican and 78% of Free Church young people think the police do a good job, only 63% of Roman Catholic young people share this view.

When the reverse perspective is examined, the figures tell the same story. In each case the percentage of Roman Catholic young people who register support for a moral code based on the law is lower by between 4 and 13% than the Anglican or Free Church figure (whichever of these two is lower on any particular item). For example, whereas 63% of Roman Catholic young people think it is wrong to buy cigarettes under age, it is 71% of Free Church young people and 75% of Anglican young people who express this opinion. So far as the police are concerned 14% of Roman Catholic young people are critical, as compared with 6% of Anglican and 7% of Free Church young people.

The uncertainty figures on every item except one (buying cigarettes) show that slightly more Roman Catholic young people (between 1 and 3%) are unsure of what is right or wrong than are their Anglican or Free Church contemporaries (whichever of these has the higher percentage on a particular item).

Implications

A substantial number of young people consider that buying alcohol under the legal age is perfectly all right, and considerably less than half (41%) firmly support the present law. This implies that young people make a distinction between what is *right* and what is *legal* and, in this instance, it must be assumed that the desire to purchase alcohol is sufficiently strong to overturn the constraints of legality. In other words, the law is seen to be wrong, or certainly questionable, by the majority of teenagers because it interferes with a legitimate pleasure. A similar pattern is observable with buying cigarettes under the legal age, but on this issue more than half (57%) support the present legal position. Presumably the greater willingness to support the law over cigarettes is due, in part, to the recognition that smoking can be harmful. Health education programmes have been operating in primary schools for many years, and the connection between smoking and ill-health has been emphasised in these programmes. National No Smoking Day has been held for more than ten years, and this contrasts with Drinkwise Day which has been marked for about half that time. Moreover, while it is possible to be completely opposed to smoking, the emphasis with regard to drinking has been on moderation. Social drinking is widely accepted; social smoking much less so. These attitudes are likely to be learnt by adolescents.

The contrast in figures between shoplifting and travelling without a ticket suggests that young people may make a distinction, perhaps unconsciously, between stealing from a shopkeeper whom they can see and stealing from a faceless corporation. The sums of money involved in both cases may be similar and small but far more young people disapprove of shoplifting than of travelling without paying. Shoplifting, of course, involves the deliberate removal of an object from premises while travelling without a ticket (especially on buses) is more excusable on grounds of forgetfulness and, in any case, is unlikely to be dealt with by prosecution.

The writing of graffiti is widely accepted: 35% of the teenagers surveyed were unwilling to condemn the practice. In general graffiti contain two kinds of message, either personal declarations about an individual ('X loves Y') or tribal slogans ('United for the Cup'). Both these categories of graffiti indicate self-expression and belonging. Even negative statements ('Down with United') imply membership of a group, in this instance the rivals of United. What is clear is that graffiti-writers disregard many notions about the inviolability of ownership.

Playing truant is as widely accepted as writing graffiti. It implies two things: first, a judgement by pupils on the education they are receiving. To absent oneself from school is the sharpest possible way of indicating that education has no value. It is irrelevant to life or employment, boring or repressive; any one of these epithets is commonly used.

Second, the truant may be saying something about his or her own future. Education, though it intends to be a worthwhile activity in its own right, is future-directed. The truant is careless of the future and does not think it worth the investment of time or effort.

Cycling without lights is condemned by three-quarters (75%) of those surveyed. It is next only to shop-lifting among activities which teenagers think are wrong. Cycling without lights is life-threatening, despite its apparent triviality. It is also covered by Road Safety campaigns and Cycling Proficiency awards which have been targeted at primary schools. It is probable, therefore, that because they have been taught about it and because it is dangerous, many young people have incorporated this requirement of the law into their moral code.

The interpretation of the figures on the police can be read in the light of the statistics presented in earlier sections. Overall, 18% of these teenagers are critical of the police and only 62% think they do a good job. What is apparent, however, is that those most critical of the police are also those less likely to support a moral code based on law. Boys, for example, are both more inclined to see illegal behaviours as acceptable and to criticise the police. And the same tendency is found among atheists (as against theists and agnostics) and Roman Catholics (as against Anglican and Free Church young people). The obvious conclusion is that *anti-police sentiment* is at the root of the criticism. If criticism of the police were generated by a view of their poor performance in combatting crime, then those most likely to act illegally would be foolish to be critical.

The figures dealing with sex differences are most different with respect to cycling without lights after dark and travelling without a ticket. Both these behaviours involve a short-term risk and, since risk leads to anxiety, it is likely that personality factors militate against these activities. On the other hand, smoking has been viewed as a means of reducing anxiety, of 'calming the nerves', which for this reason may appeal more to girls than to boys, even at the expense of breaking the law. There are other factors which are possibly at work here also. First, smoking was much more a male province in the past and, because of the current stress on female equality, cigarettes may have recently become increasingly attractive to women. Second, cigarette advertising has conveyed an association between cigarettes and sophistication. Young women seeking to give evidence of their adulthood may turn to cigarettes as a sign of maturity. Third, smoking may be seen as a way of slimming or keeping slim. Whatever the causes, however, this survey identifies a worrying attraction of cigarettes to young women, an attraction which, a few years ago, seemed to be diminishing.

The age trend shows a growing willingness to break the law, but it also demonstrates a slight shift to uncertainty, and this suggests that some young people of 14 and 15 years of age are leaving their childhood opinions and moving through uncertainty towards a more liberal view of morality. Right and wrong become separate from adult rules, even if these rules carry the force of law. When these findings are taken in conjunction with chapter 7 on *Sexual Morality* it is evident that young people are undergoing complicated alterations and reorientations towards a range of personal and social issues.

Churchgoers are more in favour of the police than are non-churchgoers, perhaps because they are more likely to be victims of crime than perpetrators of it. Certainly churchgoing is associated with respect for rules and law which implies that the nature of teenage religion, fostered by churchgoing, has an element within it conducive to legal or moral restraint. We may be correct in seeing teenage religion as a manifestation of a desire for order or, alternatively, a recognition of an order whose existence depends on God. British churchgoing teenagers do not feel alienated from law and society and their sense of right and wrong finds expression in consistently lower uncertainty percentages on the seven behaviour items. Those who attend church weekly have a clearer idea of right and wrong than do non-attenders. Furthermore the very large measure of similarity between the patterns of figures for weekly churchgoers and for non-churchgoing theists suggests that the same dynamics operate in both cases.

9 Substance use

Introduction
This chapter is concerned with whether young people consider that it is right or wrong to sniff glue, use marijuana, become drunk, sniff butane gas, smoke cigarettes or use heroin. Six statements were presented and each had the form, 'It is wrong to...'. Pupils could respond by agreeing, expressing uncertainty, or disagreeing.

Overview
The great majority of young people think that it is wrong, in descending order of seriousness, to sniff glue, use heroin or sniff butane gas. A small minority disagrees. Marijuana, cigarettes and drunkenness, also in descending order of seriousness, are less widely thought to be wrong.

Table 9.1 Substance use: overview

	Agree %	Not certain %	Disagree %
It is wrong to sniff glue	81	6	13
It is wrong to use marijuana (hash or pot)	58	19	23
It is wrong to become drunk	22	17	61
It is wrong to sniff butane gas	75	12	13
It is wrong to smoke cigarettes	45	17	38
It is wrong to use heroin	79	10	11

The figures show that 81% of teenagers think it wrong to sniff glue, and that 13% disagree; 79% think it wrong to use heroin, and 11% disagree; and that 75% think it wrong to sniff butane gas, and 13% disagree.

Teenagers have very largely made up their minds about the rights and wrongs of sniffing glue. Only 6% are not sure, and this figure is one of the lowest uncertainty figures in the entire survey. Slightly larger numbers are not sure about heroin (10%) and butane gas (12%).

112

The use of marijuana is thought to be wrong by 58% and right by 23%. Smoking cigarettes is considered wrong by 45%, though a similar number (38%) disagrees. Drunkenness is wrong in the opinion of a fifth (22%) of pupils, but in this case the majority (61%) disagrees.

Pupils are most uncertain about marijuana (19%) and slightly less uncertain about cigarettes (17%) and drunkenness (17%).

Does gender make a difference?

Girls are more likely than boys to think that it is wrong to take all the substances apart from cigarettes. For example, there is a 5% gap between the sexes on the morality of glue sniffing: while 78% of boys think it is wrong, the number of girls who think so is 83%; on the other hand, there is a 10% gap between the sexes on the morality of smoking: while 50% of *boys* think it is wrong, the number of girls who do so is 40%. Both these findings are confirmed by the reverse perspective. While 14% of boys think it is all right to sniff glue, only 12% of girls agree with them. Conversely, while 43% of girls think it is all right to smoke, only 34% of boys agree.

Table 9.2   Substance use: by gender

	Male %	Female %
It is wrong to sniff glue	78	83
It is wrong to use marijuana (hash or pot)	56	60
It is wrong to become drunk	22	21
It is wrong to sniff butane gas	72	77
It is wrong to smoke cigarettes	50	40
It is wrong to use heroin	76	81

Except with regard to drunkenness the other differences are equally clear-cut. It is 81% of girls, compared with 76% of boys, who think that it is wrong to use heroin; it is 77% of girls, compared with 72% of boys, who think it is wrong to sniff butane gas; and it is 60% of girls, compared with

56% of boys, who think it is wrong to use marijuana. The reverse perspective also shows that girls are less likely than boys to agree with taking substances. While 13% of boys think it is all right to use heroin, it is 10% of girls who agree with them. While 15% of boys think it is all right to sniff butane gas, it is 11% of girls who think the same thing. Of the illegal substances marijuana finds greatest support among both sexes: a quarter of boys (25%) and a fifth of girls (20%) find nothing wrong in its use.

Drunkenness is an exception, not only because of the substantial agreement between the sexes, but also because the majority see nothing wrong with it. Only 22% of boys and 21% of girls think it is wrong and this contrasts with the 62% of boys and 61% of girls who think it is morally acceptable.

The uncertainty figures between the sexes are no more than 3% different on any item.

Does age make a difference?

As pupils become older they are less likely to consider it wrong to use any of the six substances. This is a consistent finding and applies to both perspectives.

Table 9.3   Substance use: by age

	Year 9 %	Year 10 %
It is wrong to sniff glue	82	79
It is wrong to use marijuana (hash or pot)	60	57
It is wrong to become drunk	26	17
It is wrong to sniff butane gas	76	73
It is wrong to smoke cigarettes	49	41
It is wrong to use heroin	80	77

The largest shift of opinion occurs with regard to becoming drunk and smoking cigarettes. While 26% of year nine pupils think it is wrong to become drunk, the corresponding figure has dropped sharply to 17% a year later; while just under half (49%) of year nine pupils think it is wrong to smoke cigarettes, a year later there has been an 8% drop to 41%. From the other perspective, while 56% of year nine pupils think it all right to become drunk, as many as 67% of year ten pupils take this view; while 34% of year nine pupils think it is all right to smoke, it is 43% of year ten pupils who take this view.

The drop in those thinking that glue-sniffing, using marijuana, sniffing butane gas and using heroin is wrong is at 3% in each case. Thus, 82% of year nine pupils think it is wrong to sniff glue and 79% of year ten pupils agree. With regard to marijuana, butane gas and heroin, the figures for year nine pupils are 60%, 76% and 80% respectively. The reverse perspective confirms these figures. As many as 12% of year nine pupils and 14% of year ten pupils think it is all right to sniff glue or butane gas; 19% of year nine pupils and 25% of year ten pupils think it is all right to use marijuana; 10% of year nine pupils and 13% of year ten pupils think it is all right to use heroin.

Does church attendance make a difference?

This section examines pupils' attitudes towards substance use in the light of church attendance and makes comparisons between three groups: those who never attend church, those who attend church sometimes and those who attend church nearly every week.

Table 9.4   Substance use: by church attendance

	Weekly %	Sometimes %	Never %
It is wrong to sniff glue	85	82	79
It is wrong to use marijuana (hash or pot)	65	61	55
It is wrong to become drunk	30	22	19
It is wrong to sniff butane gas	80	76	72
It is wrong to smoke cigarettes	53	46	42
It is wrong to use heroin	85	81	76

Weekly churchgoers are more likely than occasional churchgoers to consider substance use to be wrong, and

occasional churchgoers are more likely than non-attenders to
consider substance use to be wrong. This is a consistent
finding for all six substances and from both perspectives.
The ranking of substances is the same in all three groups.
Glue-sniffing is most widely, and drunkenness is least
widely, regarded as wrong. What is noticeable, though, is
that non-churchgoers differ from weekly churchgoers and
occasional churchgoers in their tolerance of soft drugs
(alcohol, nicotine and marijuana) more than they do in their
tolerance of harder substances (heroin, butane gas and glue).

The figures give the details. While 30% of weekly
churchgoers and 22% of occasional churchgoers think it is
wrong to become drunk, it is only 19% of non-churchgoers
who agree with them; while 53% of weekly churchgoers and
46% of occasional churchgoers think it is wrong to smoke
cigarettes, it is 42% of non-churchgoers who agree with
them; while 65% of weekly churchgoers and 61% of occasional churchgoers think it is wrong to use marijuana, it is
55% of non-churchgoers who agree. So far as using heroin
is concerned, 85% of weekly churchgoers and 81% of
occasional churchgoers, compared with 76% of non-
churchgoers, think it is wrong; 80% of weekly churchgoers
and 76% of occasional churchgoers, compared with 72% of
non-churchgoers, think it wrong to sniff butane gas; and
85% of weekly churchgoers and 82% of occasional churchgoers, compared with 79% of non-churchgoers, think it
wrong to sniff glue.

The reverse perspective shows that 48% of teenage
weekly churchgoers think it is all right to get drunk,
compared with 60% of occasional churchgoers and 65% of
non-churchgoers; 29% of weekly churchgoers, compared
with 35% of occasional churchgoers and 42% of non-
churchgoers, think it is all right to smoke cigarettes; 18% of
weekly churchgoers and 20% of occasional churchgoers,
compared with 25% of non-churchgoers, think it is all right
to use marijuana; 9% of weekly churchgoers and 10%
of occasional churchgoers, compared with 13% of non-
churchgoers, think it is all right to use heroin; 11% of

weekly churchgoers and 12% of occasional churchgoers, compared with 15% of non-churchgoers, think it is all right to sniff butane gas; and 10% of weekly churchgoers and 12% of occasional churchgoers, compared with 14% of non-churchgoers, think it all right to sniff glue.

Does belief in God make a difference?

We now look in detail at those who do not go to church and explore the opinions of 'theists', 'agnostics' and 'atheists' (see page 7). The analysis shows a pattern of figures similar to the previous section. Theists are generally more inclined than agnostics to see the use of substances as wrong, and agnostics are more inclined than atheists to see the use of substances as wrong.

Table 9.5   Substance use: by belief among non-churchgoers

	Theist %	Agnostic %	Atheist %
It is wrong to sniff glue	82	80	75
It is wrong to use marijuana (hash or pot)	62	57	50
It is wrong to become drunk	22	19	18
It is wrong to sniff butane gas	77	74	66
It is wrong to smoke cigarettes	45	43	40
It is wrong to use heroin	81	79	70

Thus, while 82% of theists and 80% of agnostics think it is wrong to sniff glue, the corresponding number of atheists is 75%; while 81% of theists and 79% of agnostics think it is wrong to use heroin, the corresponding number of atheists is 70%; while 77% of theists and 74% of agnostics think it is wrong to sniff butane gas, the corresponding number of atheists is 66%; while 62% of theists and 57% of agnostics think it is wrong to use marijuana, it is 50% of atheists who take this view; while 45% of theists and 43% of agnostics think smoking cigarettes is wrong, it is 40% of atheists who believe this; while 22% of theists believe it is wrong to become drunk, it is 19% of agnostics and 18% of atheists who hold this opinion.

The reverse perspective shows that, while 13% of both theists and agnostics think sniffing glue is all right, it is 16% of atheists who take this view; while 10% of theists and agnostics think it is acceptable to use heroin, it is 18% of atheists who believe this; while 14% of theists and 13% of agnostics believe sniffing butane gas is wrong, it is 19% of atheists who think this; while 21% of theists and 22% of agnostics think it is acceptable to use marijuana, it is many more atheists (30%) who think this; while 38% of theists and 40% of agnostics think smoking cigarettes is acceptable, it is 46% of atheists who think this; and while 63% of both theists and agnostics think it is all right to become drunk, it is 68% of atheists who believe this.

Does denomination make a difference?

In the previous section we looked at those who never attend church. This section examines those who attend weekly, either in an Anglican, Free Church or Roman Catholic setting.

Table 9.6 Substance use: by denomination

	Catholic %	Anglican %	Free %
It is wrong to sniff glue	81	87	90
It is wrong to use marijuana (hash or pot)	64	66	69
It is wrong to become drunk	21	31	39
It is wrong to sniff butane gas	76	86	79
It is wrong to smoke cigarettes	48	52	56
It is wrong to use heroin	83	86	87

As we have said above, if substances are ranked in order of seriousness according to the numbers who disapprove of them, then churchgoing young people, like the general population, consider glue-sniffing or heroin most wrong, followed by butane gas, marijuana, cigarettes and drunkenness. Yet with regard to every substance the opinions of Anglican and Free Church teenagers are distinct from the general population in that far more of these churchgoers, as compared with non-churchgoers, think that taking substances is wrong. Roman Catholic young people are closer in many areas to the general population, but distinct with regard to marijuana and heroin. Free Church young people are the most likely to be opposed to substances, Anglicans the next most likely and Roman Catholics the least likely. There is a single exception to this. Anglicans are clearly more opposed to sniffing butane gas than are either of the other two denominational groups.

The denominational effects can be quantified in this way: 39% of Free Church young people and 31% of Anglicans think it is wrong to become drunk, compared with only 21% of Roman Catholic young people. The opposite perspective verifies these differences. Whereas 39% of Free Church young people think that it is morally acceptable to become drunk, it is slightly more Anglicans (43%) and very many more Roman Catholics (60%). Similarly, 90% of Free Church young people and 87% of Anglicans, compared with 81% of Roman Catholics, think it is wrong to sniff glue; conversely, 8% of Free Church young people, 9% of Anglicans but 12% of Roman Catholics think the practice is morally acceptable. Smoking shows the same sort of pattern. While 56% of Free Church young people and 52% of Anglicans think it is wrong, less than half (48%) of Roman Catholic young people do so, and rather more (35%) Catholic than Anglican (29%) or Free Church young people (25%) think it is all right.

With regard to butane gas, 86% of Anglicans, compared with 79% of Free Church and 76% of Roman Catholic young people, think that it is wrong, and the reverse perspective shows that only 8% of Anglican, 12% of Free Church and 13% of Roman Catholic young people find it acceptable. Using heroin is thought to be wrong by 87% of Free Church, 86% of Anglican and 83% of Roman Catholic young people, while only 7% of Anglican, 8% of Free Church and 10% of Roman Catholic young people disagree with the majority. Using marijuana is considered wrong by 69% of Free Church, 66% of Anglican and 64% of Roman

Catholic young people, but 15% of Anglican, 18% of Free Church and 20% of Roman Catholic young people hold the opposite opinion.

Implications

Well-publicised deaths as a result of glue-sniffing have registered in the minds of young people. Most of them have decided that it is wrong, and the very small number who are uncertain (6%) suggests that enough information, from various sources, is available to allow an informed decision to be made. This makes it all the more alarming that no less than 13% think that glue-sniffing is morally acceptable. A small core of young people holds the same opinion on butane gas-sniffing and heroin.

When the figures are examined, boys more than girls, year ten pupils more than year nine pupils, non-churchgoers more than churchgoers and atheists more than theists are inclined to favour the using of dangerous substances. For example, 19% of atheists think it is all right to sniff butane gas and 18% think it is all right to use heroin. By contrast, the corresponding figures for weekly churchgoers are 8 and 9% lower. Churchgoing is therefore linked with restraint and prudential behaviour, but it is not simply the institutional influence of the church which makes this difference because theists and agnostics who do not attend church are also significantly less inclined than atheists to think the taking of dangerous substances is morally right. For example, only 10% of theists and agnostics think it is acceptable to take heroin. Theism and agnosticism *as worldviews* are quite different from atheism.

Marijuana is less addictive than heroin and less lethal than glue or butane gas. It therefore stands apart from the most dangerous substances, and young people are well enough informed on the subject to reflect these differences in their responses. Nearly a quarter (23%) think that using marijuana is perfectly all right. This figure rises to 30% among atheists and drops to 15% among Anglicans. The case for the legalisation of marijuana has not been accepted, however, because 50% or more in all groups think that taking it is wrong. For example, at the extremes, 50% of atheists and 69% of Free Church young people reject the rightness of using marijuana. No doubt, if marijuana *were* legalised, fewer young people would consider its use wrong, but it is virtually inconceivable that the law would be changed to allow the sale of marijuana to those *under* sixteen years of age since that would make it more accessible than ordinary nicotine-based cigarettes. The situation following legalisation would be similar to that which obtains with cigarettes. There would be a percentage of teenagers who would want to gain access to marijuana even if it were banned to their age group, and who would see nothing wrong in doing so. Judging by the figures in chapter 8 on *Right and Wrong*, we estimate that less than 10% of teenagers would fall into this category. What this means is that, if marijuana were legalised, less than 10% of those who now think it wrong would change their minds.

Smoking is a controversial matter. The percentage of pupils who think that it is wrong is 7% greater than the percentage who think it is right. In a situation where the balance of opinion is even we may expect the *status quo* to persist. The position of cigarettes in this set of substances is unusual because girls are less likely to think it wrong than are boys. However, other surveys have shown that there are class differentials in the incidence of smoking and that higher social classes have reduced their cigarette intake in response to health warnings but that lower social classes have not. Nevertheless, if anti-smoking campaigns have been effective in one social group, it is difficult to see that a prolonged health education thrust in schools would fail completely among other social groups. This must particularly be so since women smoke less during pregnancy when the health risks are most pronounced. Thus, though we may expect the *status quo* to continue, an important shift against cigarettes would take place if adolescent girls could be persuaded to change their habits.

It is probable that smoking is attractive to adolescent girls because it conveys an impression of adulthood and at the same time has a calming effect and reduces appetite, thereby helping slimmers. Yet it also carries well-established health risks. The 43% of girls who think it is morally acceptable to smoke must make their decision in the light of its short-term benefits and its social usefulness. There are, of course, short-term benefits (for example, the sense of euphoria or the 'high' or 'good trip') to be had from glue-sniffing and heroin, but these have serious long-term detrimental effects and little or no social usefulness, and for this reason are overwhelmingly rejected by the bulk of the teenage population. This implies that the morality of substance use is reached by a calculation involving these factors: that right and wrong are not assessed by reference to an absolute standard but by an interplay between long and short-term effects and social utility.

Drunkenness is morally acceptable to the great majority of British teenagers. Alcohol, like smoking, has a social utility and few long-term adverse effects, provided it is taken in moderation. Though some churchgoers are teetotal, many draw a distinction between drunkenness and social drinking by condemning the first and approving the second. An 8% gap between weekly churchgoers and the general population on the wrongness of drunkenness is therefore noticeable in these figures, but this gap is not as big as it is on some of the other moral issues reported elsewhere in this book.

The figures show that churchgoers and non-churchgoing theists are the two groups of young people most opposed to drugs. This suggests that young people can be persuaded to toughen their stance against substance abuse. Churchgoers are subject to the same social influences as their peers, but because of the support and teaching they receive from their churches and because of their basic beliefs about life, they are able to stand against the drug culture more strongly. Non-churchgoing theists are opposed to drugs simply because they see the world as a different kind of place from their non-churchgoing atheistic contemporaries.

10 Leisure

Introduction

This chapter deals with young people's use of leisure time. We put forward eight statements, each dealing with a different aspect of leisure. These were, 'I often hang about with my friends doing nothing in particular', 'I wish I had more things to do in my leisure time' and 'In my area there are lots of things for young people to do in their leisure time'. Two items dealt with youth centres, 'I am frightened of going to a youth centre' and 'My youth centre is boring' and three with parents, 'My parents prefer me to stay in as much as possible', 'My parents allow me to do what I like in my leisure time' and 'My parents do not agree with most of the things I do in my leisure time.'

Overview

Two-thirds of teenagers (67%) spend time hanging around doing nothing in particular and a third (34%) find their youth centres boring. According to 65% of 13 to 15 year olds their parents are quite happy for them to go out rather than stay at home as much as possible.

In detail, whereas two-thirds (67%) of teenagers often hang around aimlessly, just under a quarter (23%) are more purposefully engaged, and nearly the same number (27%) think that there are lots of things for young people to do in their area. More than half (57%) do not think the provision of leisure facilities in their area is satisfactory, and a nearly identical number (58%) wish that they had more to do with their leisure time.

Only 8% of teenagers are frightened of going out to the youth centre (though a further 16% are uncertain about this) but, when they get to the centre, 34% find it boring and only 24% like it. A large group of 42% is uncertain about whether the youth centre is boring or not.

Table 10.1   Leisure: overview

	Agree %	Not certain %	Disagree %
I often hang around with my friends doing nothing in particular	67	10	23
In my area there are lots of things for young people to do in their leisure time	27	16	57
I wish I had more things to do in my leisure time	58	15	27
I am frightened of going to a youth centre	8	16	76
My youth centre is boring	34	42	24
My parents prefer me to stay in as much as possible	17	18	65
My parents allow me to do what I like in my leisure time	49	17	34
My parents do not agree with most of the things I do in my leisure time	28	18	54

Parents in only 17% of cases want their teenagers to stay in as much as possible; 18% are uncertain. Nearly half of the teenagers (49%) agreed that their parents allowed them to do as they wanted in their leisure time, though 34% disagreed with this and felt that their parents exercised some control even over leisure activities. A smaller number (17%) were uncertain about this. Relations with parents over the use of leisure time are not always harmonious. More than one in four teenagers (28%) reported that their parents did not agree with their use of leisure time, but this figure must be set against the more than one in two (54%) whose parents supported the leisure activities of their children.

Does gender make a difference?

Differences between males and females show up in three main ways. First, more girls than boys tend to hang around with their friends doing nothing in particular: whereas 62% of boys agree with the statement, the figure for girls is 71%. This tendency is confirmed by the reverse perspective: 27% of boys do not hang around doing nothing in particular, compared with 20% of girls. Second, more girls are critical of the leisure facilities in their area than are boys. Whereas 32% of boys think there are lots of things to do, the figure for girls is only 22%, and the reverse perspective again confirms these findings (64% of girls do not think there is enough to do in their area, compared with 51% of boys). Youth centres, it is true, are found boring by more boys (37%) than girls (32%), but the large number of uncertain boys (40%) and even larger number of uncertain girls (44%) implies, as we shall suggest at the end of this chapter, that many young people either do not have access to a youth centre or have not spent much time there. Third, parents tend to be more concerned to control their daughters' use of leisure. While over half of boys (53%) say their parents allow them to do as they please in their leisure time, it is only 47% of girls who say this. Again the reverse perspective also confirms this finding: whereas 30% of boys are not allowed to do as they want during leisure time, it is 37% of girls who say this.

Table 10.2   Leisure: by gender

	Male %	Female %
I often hang around with my friends doing nothing in particular	62	71
In my area there are lots of things for young people to do in their leisure time	32	22
I wish I had more things to do in my leisure time	56	59
I am frightened of going to a youth centre	8	8
My youth centre is boring	37	32
My parents prefer me to stay in as much as possible	16	19
My parents allow me to do what I like in my leisure time	53	47
My parents do not agree with most of the things I do in my leisure time	29	27

Other differences between male and female comments on leisure time are minor and amount to no more than 4% on any figure. For example, 16% of boys say their parents prefer them to stay in as much as possible, compared with 19% of girls; 56% of boys and 59% of girls wish they had more things to do with their leisure time and 8% of both boys and girls are frightened to go out to their youth centres.

Does age make a difference?

The age trend with regard to use of leisure time is not strongly marked. All the comparisons between year nine and year ten pupils vary by no more than 3%, with two exceptions. There is a strong indication that pupils, as they get older, find their leisure facilities increasingly inadequate. As many as 31% of year nine pupils say there are lots of things to do for young people in their area, but by the time year ten is reached, only 23% of them agree with this.

Table 10.3   Leisure: by age

	Year 9 %	Year 10 %
I often hang around with my friends doing nothing in particular	67	66
In my area there are lots of things for young people to do in their leisure time	31	23
I wish I had more things to do in my leisure time	58	58
I am frightened of going to a youth centre	8	8
My youth centre is boring	32	37
My parents prefer me to stay in as much as possible	16	18
My parents allow me to do what I like in my leisure time	49	50
My parents do not agree with most of the things I do in my leisure time	27	30

The opposite perspective underlines this shift. While 53% of year nine pupils think there are not enough things to do in their area, this figure has risen to 62% a year later. The youth centre is one of the main butts of this criticism. While 32% of year nine pupils think it is boring, the figure rises to 37% for year ten pupils; similarly 26% of year nine pupils

do not think their youth centre is boring, as opposed to 20%
of year ten pupils.

Does church attendance make a difference?

It would be logical to expect that churchgoing young people,
to the extent that churchgoing can be classified as a leisure
activity, would have slightly less unoccupied leisure time
than do their non-churchgoing friends. The figures show this
to be the case. Whereas 60% of weekly churchgoers often
hang around with their friends doing nothing in particular,
the comparable figures for occasional attenders is 65% and
for non-attenders is 69%. The reverse perspective confirms
this: while 29% of weekly attenders do not hang around
doing nothing in particular, 24% of occasional attenders and
21% of non-attenders say the same.

Table 10.4   Leisure: by church attendance

	Weekly %	Sometimes %	Never %
I often hang around with my friends doing nothing in particular	60	65	69
In my area there are lots of things for young people to do in their leisure time	29	28	26
I wish I had more things to do in my leisure time	55	58	58
I am frightened of going to a youth centre	9	9	7
My youth centre is boring	25	33	37
My parents prefer me to stay in as much as possible	20	18	16
My parents allow me to do what I like in my leisure time	40	47	53
My parents do not agree with most of the things I do in my leisure time	23	25	31

A quarter of weekly churchgoers (25%), as compared
with 37% of non-attenders and 33% of occasional attenders,
are inclined to find the youth centre boring, but a higher
percentage of weekly churchgoers (20%) find their parents
prefer them to stay indoors than is the case with occasional

attenders (18%) and non-attenders (16%). The opposite perspective confirms both these findings: 31% of weekly churchgoers, 23% of occasional attenders and 23% of non-attenders find their youth centre entertaining; 59% of weekly churchgoers, 64% of occasional attenders and 67% of non-attenders say that their parents prefer them not to stay at home.

In connection with parental preference for children to stay at home, weekly churchgoers are more likely than non-churchgoers to find parents putting limits on the way leisure time is spent. Forty per cent of weekly churchgoers, 47% of occasional attenders and 53% of non-churchgoers say their parents allow them to do as they like and, from the opposite perspective, these findings are reiterated: 43% of weekly churchgoers, 36% of occasional attenders and 30% of non-churchgoers are not allowed to do as they please during leisure times.

Weekly churchgoers are less likely to be in conflict with their parents over the use of leisure time. While 23% of weekly church attenders say their parents do not agree with most of their leisure activities, the figures for occasional attenders is 25% and for non-attenders is 31%; these figures are confirmed by the reverse perspective where the respective figures are 59%, 57% and 51%.

The actual assessment by weekly churchgoers and non-churchgoers of the facilities provided by their areas does not vary very much. While 29% of weekly churchgoers think there are lots of things for young people to do nearby, the figure for occasional attenders is 28% and for non-attenders is 26%. When the reverse perspective is used, the figures confirm this judgment. While 54% of weekly churchgoers and 57% of occasional attenders do not think there is much to do in their area, the figure for non-attenders is 58%. In its pattern this set of figures is similar to that found in responses to the statement, 'I wish I had more things to do in my leisure time' where 55% of weekly churchgoers wish for more things to do and 58% of the other two groups feel the same. Similarly, while 28% of weekly churchgoers clearly have enough to do in their leisure time, the figure for occasional attenders is 27% and for non-attenders is 26%.

Does belief in God make a difference?

We now turn attention to those young people who do not attend church and compare the attitudes towards leisure held by three distinct groups: 'theists', 'agnostics' and 'atheists' (see page 7). The figures show that, with regard to the use of leisure time, these three groups differ in two main ways.

Table 10.5   Leisure: by belief among non-churchgoers

	Theist %	Agnostic %	Atheist %
I often hang around with my friends doing nothing in particular	70	69	68
In my area there are lots of things for young people to do in their leisure time	27	26	25
I wish I had more things to do in my leisure time	62	58	56
I am frightened of going to a youth centre	8	7	6
My youth centre is boring	36	35	39
My parents prefer me to stay in as much as possible	17	16	16
My parents allow me to do what I like in my leisure time	50	51	57
My parents do not agree with most of the things I do in my leisure time	30	28	34

First, the theists are more inclined to mention parental control of the use of leisure time: while 50% of theists say their parents allow them to do what they like during leisure time, the figure for agnostics is 51% and for atheists is 57%. The reverse perspective confirms this set of opinions. While 33% of theists say their parents do not allow them to do as they like in their leisure time, only 31% of agnostics and 28% of atheists say the same thing. Following on from the greater parental control over theists, theists are less likely than atheists (30% as against 34%) to say, 'My parents do not agree with most of the things I do in my leisure time'.

Second, theists have a tendency to wish they had more to do in their leisure time. While 62% of theists wish this, the figure for agnostics is 58% and for atheists is 56%; the reverse perspective does not confirm this, however, and shows that 24% of theists do not want more to do in their leisure time, compared with 25% of agnostics and 29% of atheists.

The other figures of comparison between the three groups do not vary by more than 5%, and usually by less. For example, 36% of theists, 35% of agnostics and 39% of atheists find their youth centre boring and 24% of atheists and theists and 21% of agnostics do not find their youth centre boring.

Does denomination make a difference?

Having looked in the previous section at young people who never attend church, we turn attention now to those who attend weekly. We try to discover whether denominational identity is linked in any systematic way with the use of leisure time.

Table 10.6   Leisure: by denomination

	Catholic %	Anglican %	Free %
I often hang around with my friends doing nothing in particular	62	56	62
In my area there are lots of things for young people to do in their leisure time	28	33	31
I wish I had more things to do in my leisure time	58	49	59
I am frightened of going to a youth centre	9	10	6
My youth centre is boring	33	21	22
My parents prefer me to stay in as much as possible	22	19	16
My parents allow me to do what I like in my leisure time	35	43	41
My parents do not agree with most of the things I do in my leisure time	23	20	22

The figures show that, of the three denominational groups, the Anglican young people are the most contented with their leisure facilities and activities. Compared with the other two groups, the Anglican young people hang around doing nothing in particular less frequently, more of them think there is plenty to do in their area, they are less likely to wish for more things to do in their leisure time, they are least likely to think their youth centre is boring, they are most frequently allowed to do as they like by their parents and they are least likely to find their parents disagreeing with the way they use their leisure time.

The figures are as follows: while 56% of Anglican young people often hang around doing nothing in particular, 62% of Free Church and Roman Catholic young people say the same; whereas 28% of Roman Catholic and 31% of Free Church adolescents say there is plenty to do in their area, it is 33% of Anglican young people who give this response; whereas 59% of Free Church and 58% of Roman Catholic young people wish they had more things to do with their leisure time, it is only 49% of Anglicans who express this view. As the comparison continues, the statistics largely point in the same direction: whereas 33% of Roman Catholic and 22% of Free Church young people say their youth centre is boring, it is 21% of Anglicans who take this view; whereas 35% of Roman Catholic and 41% of Free Church young people say their parents allow them to do what they like, it is 43% of Anglicans who are able to say this; and whereas 23% of Roman Catholic and 22% of Free Church young people say their parents do not agree with most things they do in their leisure time, it is 20% of Anglicans who make this statement.

The reverse perspective substantially confirms these findings. It is only on two matters that there is a minor discrepancy. While 61% of Anglican young people say their parents *do* agree with their use of leisure time, the figure for Free Church young people stands at 64%; for Roman Catholics it is at 58%. Similarly, the percentage of Free Church and Anglican young people who enjoy their youth

club is identical at 35%, considerably higher than that for
Roman Catholics who stand at 21%.

Implications

There is a sharp difference between the quarter of young
people who are satisfied with their leisure facilities and who
do not often hang around doing nothing in particular and the
nearly two-thirds who are aimless and apparently starved of
enough to do. It is presumably among the aimless teenagers
that we should locate the third who are bored with youth
centres. Equally probably there is likely to be friction
between parents and aimless teenagers about how leisure
time should be used. Altogether 28% of young people report
friction between their parents and themselves about the use
of leisure time.

The survey suggests that youth centres are not perceived
as being interesting to the majority of young people; only
24% of young people give them an approval rating. When
we put this finding alongside the figures on under age
buying of alcohol and cigarettes in chapter 8, *Right and
Wrong,* and young people's desire for a *Listening Ear*
(chapter 2), it is probable that the failure of youth leaders to
be perceived as counsellors and the frequent banning of
smoking and drinking at youth clubs make them neither one
thing nor the other in the eyes of teenagers. They cannot
receive help with their personal problems and they cannot
emulate the adult world of the pub or night club. Moreover,
the extremely high uncertainty figure about 'my youth
centre', more than twice the comparable figure for any of
the other items in this chapter, suggests that young people
do not know enough about their youth centre to comment.
Either there are no youth centres in some districts or young
people in large numbers have never attended. Certainly this
interpretation would fit with the complaint by 57% of young
people that there are not enough things to do in their area.

The problems young people have with the use of their
leisure time are not directly related to their parents. Most
parents (65%) do not prefer their teenagers to stay indoors

and nearly half (49%) allow teenagers to do as they please. Moreover, the problems cannot entirely be related to the amenities of the area since, whether we examine the global figures or the figures on sex or age differences, there are always more young people who say there are lots of things to do in their area than there are who say they do not hang around doing nothing in particular. It is the age trend figures which are most revealing. While 67% of pupils in year nine hang about with nothing much to do, the comparable figure for year ten pupils is 66%. Yet year ten pupils complain in greater numbers that there is not much to do in their area (53%, compared with 62%). What seems to have happened is that young people are in the process of orientating themselves towards their peer group in loose social networks. Whether there is more or less to do in the area, young people still hang around doing nothing in particular.

Girls tend to hang around with their friends more than do boys and to be more inclined to find youth clubs boring. These tendencies must relate to divergencies between girls and boys in their social development or to the different rate of male and female maturation. At the same time as girls and boys show their social dissimilarity, parents treat sons and daughters differently. Parents prefer their daughters to stay at home and are less likely to let girls do as they please. Whatever the canons of political correctness may dictate, these differences in gender preference and in gender treatment by parents suggest that distinctions in sex roles are reinforced rather than obliterated in the teenage years.

Objective assessments of the quality of amenities in a neighbourhood only vary slightly among weekly church attenders, occasional attenders and non-attenders. But the subjective assessment of whether the youth centre is boring is more marked (12% difference between weekly churchgoers and non-attenders). Churchgoers are happier with the facilities available to them and are a little less disposed to aimless social behaviour. This suggests either that church youth centres are popular or that churchgoers are more willing to be involved in the semi-organised activities of secular youth clubs.

11   Religious beliefs

Introduction

In this chapter we describe some of the key religious beliefs held by young people. To sample these beliefs we put forward seven statements. 'I believe in God' reveals the distribution of theists, agnostics and atheists and has been used elsewhere in this survey to isolate these three groups so that their characteristics could be described; the analysis used in this chapter, however, is different in that it makes use of the *whole* sample and not simply those who do not belong to a church or other religious group. As we point out in the *Introduction*, approximately 54% of the total sample do not consider themselves to belong to a church or religious group; the other 46% are included in the overview given below. 'I believe God punishes people who do wrong' gives an indication about the sort of God some young people believe in. 'I believe that God made the world in six days and rested on the seventh' shows how widespread is a traditional concept of God as Creator. Two items were focused on Jesus Christ: 'I believe that Jesus Christ is the Son of God' and 'I believe that Jesus Christ really rose from the dead'. The item, 'I think Christianity is the only true religion' explored one way in which Christianity as a whole is understood by teenagers. 'I believe in life after death' completes this set of statements.

Overview

The religious beliefs of young people vary widely. On the basic matter of whether a God exists or not, significant percentages adopt each of the three main positions. Nearly two out of five (39%) are theists and a similar number (35%) are agnostics. Atheists amount to a quarter (26%). The connection between belief in God and morality is demonstrated by the fifth (19%) who believe that God punishes wrongdoers. On the other hand, 39% are uncertain about this and 42% definitely disagree with this view.

Table 11.1   Religious beliefs: overview

	Agree %	Not certain %	Disagree %
I believe in God	39	35	26
I believe God punishes people who do wrong	19	39	42
I believe that Jesus Christ is the Son of God	47	34	19
I believe that Jesus Christ really rose from the dead	30	43	27
I believe in life after death	41	41	18
I believe that God made the world in six days and rested on the seventh	17	42	41
I think Christianity is the only true religion	16	42	42

Whether or not God is a moral being, the traditional concept of God as Creator of the world in six days is held by more than one in six (17%), but two out of five (42%) are unsure of this and the remaining 41% reject the idea entirely.

Oddly enough, the teenagers believing that Jesus Christ is the Son of God (47%) considerably outnumber those who believe in God (39%). A third of pupils (34%) are uncertain that Jesus is the Son of God and the remaining fifth (19%) are sure they disbelieve this. Roughly a third (30%) believe, and slightly fewer disbelieve (27%), in the literal resurrection of Christ, but the largest percentage (43%) is unsure.

The view that Christianity is the only true religion is held by only 16% of teenagers and rejected by 42%. The remaining 42% are uncertain about this. Whatever pupils believe about the exclusive truth of Christianity, however, it is clear that general religious beliefs are widely held because 41% believe in life after death and only 18% reject belief in the possibility of personal immortality; 41% are agnostic on the matter.

Does gender make a difference?

There are marked differences between teenage males and females on all the religious beliefs sampled here. The most distinct differences concern belief in God, beliefs about Jesus and beliefs about the exclusive truth of Christianity. While 34% of boys believe in God, the number of girls who believe is higher at 44%, and this tendency is confirmed by percentages relating to disbelief; whereas 20% of girls are atheists, the figure for boys is 33%.

Table 11.2   Religious beliefs: by gender

	Male %	Female %
I believe in God	34	44
I believe God punishes people who do wrong	18	20
I believe that Jesus Christ is the Son of God	43	52
I believe that Jesus Christ really rose from the dead	27	33
I believe in life after death	39	42
I believe that God made the world in six days and rested on the seventh	15	19
I think Christianity is the only true religion	18	14

Girls are also more likely than boys to believe that Jesus is the Son of God. While 43% of boys believe this, a further 9% of girls believe (52%). Similarly, when the reverse figures for disbelief are examined, it is the boys who are more inclined to reject faith: whereas only 13% of girls do not believe Jesus is the Son of God, nearly a quarter of boys (24%) come to the same conclusion.

Belief in the literal resurrection of Jesus follows the same pattern. While just over a quarter of boys (27%) accept traditional Christian teaching on this matter, a third of girls (33%) agree with them. Conversely, while 21% of girls reject the literal resurrection, the number of boys who do so is considerably higher at 34%. Where girls are *less* traditional, however, is in relation to the exclusive truth claims of Christianity. While 18% of boys think that Christianity is the only true religion, the comparable number of girls only reaches 14%, and the reverse perspective confirms this tendency because, while 42% of boys deny that Christianity is the only true religion, the number of girls who do so is slightly higher at 43%.

The remaining items all show another pattern. While there are similarities in the number of girls and boys who agree with the statements, the gap between girls and boys opens up in the area of disbelief. Thus, while 39% of boys and 42% of girls agree that there is life after death, only 14% of girls, as compared with 23% of boys, disbelieve this. In the same way, while 15% of boys and 19% of girls believe God made the world in six days, the percentage of girls who disbelieve this (34%) is considerably less than that for boys (48%) who disbelieve. While 18% of boys and 20% of girls agree that God punishes people who do wrong, the 39% of girls who disbelieve this are considerably outnumbered by the 46% of boys who do so.

The uncertainty figures also show an interesting pattern. Girls are consistently more uncertain than boys. Whereas 33% of boys are uncertain about believing in God, the figure for girls is 36%; while 36% of boys are not sure if God punishes those who do wrong, 41% of girls are uncertain; while 37% of boys are uncertain if God made the world in six days, 46% of girls express uncertainty; while 33% of boys are unsure if Jesus is the Son of God, it is 35% of girls who take this view; while 39% of boys are unsure about the literal resurrection, it is 47% of girls who register uncertainty; while 38% of boys are unsure about life after death, it is 44% of girls who share this uncertainty with them and, while 40% of boys are unsure if Christianity is the only true religion, it is 43% of girls who express a similar viewpoint.

Does age make a difference?

The age trend shows a slight but consistent shift away from belief. Whereas 41% of year nine pupils believe in God, by year ten this figure has dropped to 37% and the reverse perspective shows an increase in those who do not believe in God in the same period from 24% to 28%.

Table 11.3   Religious beliefs: by age

	Year 9 %	Year 10 %
I believe in God	41	37
I believe God punishes people who do wrong	20	18
I believe that Jesus Christ is the Son of God	49	46
I believe that Jesus Christ really rose from the dead	32	28
I believe in life after death	40	41
I believe that God made the world in six days and rested on the seventh	18	16
I think Christianity is the only true religion	17	16

Whereas 20% of year nine pupils believe God punishes people who do wrong, the figure drops to 18% in year ten and the reverse perspective shows a rise in the number who do not believe God punishes wrongdoers from 40% to 44%. So far as the traditional view of creation is concerned, the figure for pupils who believe drops from 18% in year nine to 16% in year ten, and the figure of those who disbelieve rises in the same period from 39% to 43%.

The two items on Jesus Christ show a similar erosion. While 49% of year nine pupils believe that Jesus is the Son of God, by year ten this figure has fallen to 46%, and there is a similar 3% shift in the number of those who disbelieve (17% in year nine and 20% in year ten). Faith in the literal resurrection drops slightly more sharply. In year nine 32% of pupils believe that Jesus rose from the dead and a year later only 28% believe. At the other end of the scale, 25% of year nine pupils do not believe in the resurrection and this figure rises to 30% a year later.

Confidence in the exclusive claims of Christianity also diminishes. In year nine 17% of pupils accept that Christianity is the only true religion, but a year later this figure has fallen to 16%. Similarly, the number of pupils who reject the unique truth claims of Christianity rises from 40% in year nine to 44% in year ten.

Even belief in an after life, which is not a belief tied specifically to Christianity, shows signs of diminishing, though the figures are not clear-cut. In year nine 40% of pupils believe in life after death, but by year ten 41% hold this opinion; but there is also a countervailing tendency as the reverse perspective shows because, while 18% of pupils do not believe in life after death in year nine, it is 19% who disbelieve in year ten.

The uncertainty figures show a difference of no more than 3% on any item and a general tendency for less uncertainty to be expressed in year ten. The only exception to this rule is towards the statement, 'I believe in God', where there is a rise in uncertainty from 10% in year nine to 13% in year ten.

Does church attendance make a difference?

Church attendance and religious beliefs are, as might be expected, strongly connected. A far larger proportion of weekly churchgoers consistently holds traditional Christian opinions than is the case with occasional churchgoers or non-churchgoers, and the percentages associated with occasional churchgoers are intermediate between the other two groups. Nevertheless there are some weekly churchgoers who do not hold traditional Christian beliefs and some non-churchgoers who do.

While 84% of weekly churchgoers and 50% of occasional churchgoers believe in God, the figure for non-churchgoers is 23%, and this finding is confirmed by the reverse perspective which shows that, while 2% of weekly churchgoers and 12% of occasional churchgoers do not believe in God, the percentage of non-churchgoers who do not believe in God reaches 40%.

The concept of God held by the three different categories is revealed by their response to the next statement. While 30% of weekly churchgoers believe that God punishes those who do wrong, 22% of occasional churchgoers and only

13% of non-churchgoers believe this. The reverse perspective shows that 34% of weekly churchgoers do not believe
God punishes wrongdoers, as compared with 34% of
occasional churchgoers and 51% of non-churchgoers.

Table 11.4   Religious beliefs: by church attendance

	Weekly %	Sometimes %	Never %
I believe in God	84	50	23
I believe God punishes people who do wrong	30	22	13
I believe that Jesus Christ is the Son of God	85	58	32
I believe that Jesus Christ really rose from the dead	75	37	16
I believe in life after death	60	43	35
I believe that God made the world in six days and rested on the seventh	47	20	9
I think Christianity is the only true religion	36	18	11

Of those who attend church weekly 47% believe in the
traditional concept of God as Creator in six days. This
opinion is only held by 20% of occasional attenders and 9%
of non-churchgoers. The opposite perspective shows that a
fifth (20%) of weekly attenders reject the traditional concept,
and this position is shared by 31% of occasional churchgoers
and 52% of non-churchgoers.

Churchgoers consistently are more likely to believe the
historic teaching of the church about Jesus Christ. While
85% of weekly churchgoers and 58% of occasional attenders
believe that Jesus is the Son of God, the figure for non-
churchgoers is 32%; the reverse perspective confirms this
finding clearly. While 3% of weekly churchgoers and 9% of
occasional attenders do not believe in the resurrection, the
figure for non-churchgoers is very much higher at 29%.
Similarly, while 75% of weekly churchgoers and 37% of
occasional churchgoers believe Jesus really rose from the
dead, the figure for non-churchgoers is only 16%. In the
reverse perspective, while only 4% of weekly churchgoers
and 15% of occasional churchgoers do not believe in the

literal resurrection, it is 40% of non-churchgoers who disbelieve.

Of weekly churchgoers 36% believe that Christianity is the only true religion. This opinion is shared by 18% of occasional churchgoers and, surprisingly, by 11% of non-churchgoers. On the other hand, 30% of weekly churchgoers do not think that Christianity is the only true religion, and they are joined in this view by 39% of occasional church-goers and 47% of non-churchgoers.

Belief in life after death is held by 60% of weekly churchgoers, by 43% of occasional churchgoers and by 35% of non-churchgoers. Reversing the perspective 9% of weekly churchgoers do not believe in life after death, and this opinion is shared by 12% of occasional churchgoers and nearly a quarter of non-churchgoers (24%).

The uncertainty figures show that weekly churchgoers are the least uncertain group in their religious opinions and that, on most topics, the occasional churchgoers are the most uncertain group. Thus, while 14% of weekly church-goers and 37% of non-churchgoers are uncertain about the existence of God, the figure for occasional attenders is 38%; while 19% of weekly churchgoers and 24% of non-churchgoers are uncertain if God punishes people who do wrong, the figure for occasional churchgoers is 34%; while 33% of weekly churchgoers and 39% of non-churchgoers are not sure whether or not to believe God made the world in six days, nearly half (49%) of occasional churchgoers confess to similar uncertainty; while 21% of weekly church-goers and 44% of non-churchgoers are unsure about the resurrection, the figure for occasional attenders is 48%; while 34% of weekly church attenders and 42% of non-churchgoers think Christianity is the only true religion, the figure for occasional attenders is 43%. Even on the matter of life after death the same pattern is observable. While 31% of weekly churchgoers and 41% of non-churchgoers are uncertain about an afterlife, the figure for occasional churchgoers is 45%. The only exception to this general trend is that, while 12% of weekly churchgoers are unsure if Jesus is the Son of God, the figures for occasional churchgoers and non-churchgoers are 33% and 39% respectively.

Does belief in God make a difference?

We now look in more detail at the 53% of the sample who do not attend a church and explore the differences in beliefs of three distinct groups: 'theists', 'agnostics' and 'atheists' (see page 7).

Table 11.5 Religious beliefs: by belief among non-churchgoers

	Theist %	Agnostic %	Atheist %
I believe in God	–	–	–
I believe God punishes people who do wrong	35	9	4
I believe that Jesus Christ is the Son of God	77	29	10
I believe that Jesus Christ really rose from the dead	52	8	4
I believe in life after death	58	30	26
I believe that God made the world in six days and rested on the seventh	25	5	3
I think Christianity is the only true religion	21	9	7

In general the profile of the theists is similar to that of churchgoers. The profile of agnostics is consistently somewhere between that of theists and atheists. While 35% of theists believe God punishes people who do wrong, it is 9% of agnostics and 4% of atheists who believe this. While 25% of theists believe God made the world in six days, it is 5% of agnostics and 3% of atheists who believe this. While over three quarters (77%) of theists believe Jesus Christ is the Son of God, the figures for agnostics and atheists are 29% and 10% respectively. While 52% of theists believe in the resurrection of Christ, the figure for agnostics is 8% and for atheists 4%. While 21% of theists think Christianity is the only true religion, only 9% of agnostics think this, as compared with 7% of atheists. Belief in life after death is widespread in all three groups. While 58% of theists and

30% of agnostics believe in this, it is unexpected to find that 26% of atheists also take this view.

The reverse perspective confirms these findings. While 26% of theists do not believe God punishes people who do wrong, the number of agnostics who do not believe is higher at 35%, and the number of atheists is higher still at 82%. Similarly, 22% of theists do not believe God made the world in six days, as compared with 40% of agnostics and 81% of atheists. Theists and agnostics are similar in their disbelief that Jesus is the Son of God: 3% of theists and 8% of agnostics disbelieve, compared with 62% of atheists. Similarly, 7% of theists and 20% of agnostics do not believe in the resurrection, compared with 76% of atheists. So far as the unique truth claims of Christianity are concerned, 35% of theists and 37% of agnostics deny them, compared with 64% of atheists. Belief in life after death is only denied by 9% of theists and 14% of agnostics who contrast with the 44% of atheists who make a similar denial.

Does denomination make a difference?

The previous section looked at young people who never attend church. This section examines those who attend weekly, either in an Anglican, Free Church or Roman Catholic setting.

Table 11.6   Religious beliefs: by denomination

	Catholic %	Anglican %	Free %
I believe in God	88	87	85
I believe God punishes people who do wrong	24	30	35
I believe that Jesus Christ is the Son of God	88	89	87
I believe that Jesus Christ really rose from the dead	78	78	78
I believe in life after death	62	59	64
I believe that God made the world in six days and rested on the seventh	35	48	60
I think Christianity is the only true religion	34	34	42

The difference between the three denominations is most noticeable in three areas. First, there is a stronger tendency for Free Church young people to believe that God punishes people who do wrong. While 35% of Free Church young people hold this view, the comparable figure for Anglicans is 30% and for Roman Catholic young people is 24%; this finding is confirmed by the reverse perspective where 28% of Free Church young people do not believe God punishes wrongdoers, while 29% of Anglican and 41% of Roman Catholic teenagers take this view. Second, there is a much stronger likelihood that Free Church young people will believe that God made the world in six days. While a third of Roman Catholic young people (35%) and nearly half of Anglican young people (48%) believe this, the figure for Free Church teenagers is as high as 60%; again the reverse perspective underlines this finding because, while 26% of Roman Catholic young people do not hold this view, the comparable figures for Anglican and Free Church teenagers are 17% and 16% respectively. Third, there is a greater probability that Free Church teenagers will think that Christianity is the only true religion. More than two out of five Free Church teenagers (42%) take this stance, as compared with a third (34%) of Anglican and Roman Catholic teenagers. However, in this instance the reverse perspective shows that the situation is more complex. We discuss this at the end of the chapter. While 26% of Free Church young people do not believe that Christianity is the only true religion, more Anglicans (34%) and fewer Catholics (25%) think this.

Agreement and disagreement with all the other statements show great similarity. For instance, 78% of the young people in each of the denominational groups believe that Jesus really rose from the dead, and the other figures vary by no more than five percentage points.

Implications

The distribution of theists, agnostics and atheists is reasonably even, though there is a predominance of theists. Even in the materialistic and largely secular society of modern Britain, theism is significantly more acceptable than atheism and, though these figures show a more sceptical population than would be the case if the previous generation were surveyed, it is clear that both the churches and religious educators ought to be able to gain a hearing from the young.

Belief in God is not as simple as it might seem and nor is atheism. This is shown in three ways. First, more young people believe that Jesus is the Son of God than believe in God (table 11.1). The most sensible explanation of this discrepancy is that the term 'Son of God' is understood as a title or as religious language to convey the special character of Christ.

Second, while 35% of theists in table 11.5 believe that God punishes those who do wrong, as compared with 4% of atheists (a finding in itself which needs explanation), the percentage of weekly churchgoers who believe God punishes wrongdoers in table 11.4 is *lower* than this. It is 30%. This suggests that churchgoers have a view of a more tolerant God than do theists. This is borne out by the reverse perspective. While 34% of weekly churchgoers believe that God definitely does not punish wrongdoers, the figure for theists is lower at 26%. Since the sample has deliberately omitted Buddhists, Muslims, Jews, Hindus, Mormons, Hari Krishna and Jehovah's Witnesses, those who remain are not theists from an alternative world religion or a sect. These theists are, from the pattern of the figures, Christian in orientation. More than a fifth (21%) of them believe Christianity is the only true religion and more than half (52%) believe Jesus rose from the dead.

Third, the presence of atheists who believe that God punishes people who do wrong either suggests that atheism is in some cases to be understood as a denial of a personal deity but an affirmation of moral law, or evidence of confusion. A similar point may be made about the atheists who believe God made the world in six days. This small group may in effect be saying, 'I don't believe in God and the kind of God I don't believe in is one who punishes wrongdoers or creates the world in six days flat'. Religious education has not aided the theists or atheists to develop a coherence of belief. However, the probability, on the basis of responses to other statements, is that we have complexity rather than confusion among some of these young people. This is because 7% of the atheists believe that Christianity is the only true religion. The most reasonable explanation of this position is that these atheists accept the Christian ethic of love but reject any idea this ethic is underwritten by a real deity.

Agnostics demonstrate their own complications in these figures. There is a contrast between the 8% of them who do not believe that Jesus is the Son of God and the 20% who do not believe in the resurrection. Moreover, the highest uncertainty figure in table 11.5 is held by the agnostics who are unsure about the truth of the resurrection. Many agnostics clearly find it more difficult to believe in the resurrection than to believe that Jesus is the Son of God. Nearly a third (30%) of agnostics believe in life after death and only 14% definitely rule this out. Many agnostics, therefore, believe that Jesus is special in some way, but balk at the idea of literal resurrection without rejecting the notion of some sort of survival beyond the grave. Just under 10% of agnostics do, however, believe in the resurrection of Christ and that God punishes wrongdoers and that Christianity is the only true religion. This section of agnostics evidently has difficulty with the concept of God rather than with miraculous events on earth.

The difference between the sexes in table 11.2 shows that females are generally more sympathetic to theism and Christianity than are males. The less expected finding is that females demonstrate a greater willingness to be inclusive than do males. The Christianity supported by females is one which is more willing to embrace the people or ideas of other faiths. Males are less inclined than females to adopt a religious stance, but if they do they are more inclined than females to adopt an exclusive view. The different ways in which males and females hold their faith is itself a matter for future research.

The age trend, which shows a slight but consistent decline in religious belief, accords with findings reported in relation to sexual morality and to ideas of right and wrong elsewhere in this book. There is shift to liberalism with age and, not surprisingly, this shift is allied to a reduction in the prevalence of religious belief.

Churchgoing teenagers, though they believe in the traditional teaching of the church much more frequently than non-attending contemporaries are, however, less than fully convinced of the great doctrines of scripture and the creeds. For example, as table 11.4 shows, 16% of weekly church-goers cannot say they believe in God and 25% are unable to affirm the literal resurrection of Christ. As many as 40% of weekly churchgoers cannot declare they are certain about an afterlife and nearly two-thirds (64%) are not sure that Christianity is the only true religion. There is room here for a thorough exposition of Christianity to young churchgoers.

Table 11.6 shows how the three denominational groups selected here compare with each other. The Free Church young people tend to be more conservative in their faith than the Roman Catholics and Anglicans, but it is notice-able how churchgoers in all three contexts have grasped and accepted the literal truth of the resurrection of Christ. Yet, there are three insights the figures give into the way denominational emphases affect the faith of the young. First, the Roman Catholics are much less inclined than the others to accept that God punishes wrongdoers. It is not clear why this should be, unless it is related to the practice of confession and absolution. Second, there is a large group of non-exclusive Anglicans. More than a third (34%) of Anglicans assert that Christianity is not the only true religion. This suggests that some Anglicans, while they hold their credal faith in the same way as the Roman Catholic and Free Church young people, are distinct in that they are unwilling to pass judgement on other religions. Third, the debate between creationism and evolution looks like a

Protestant phenomenon. Roman Catholics are more uncertain than the other groups about the matter and more than a quarter (26%) definitely reject the traditional biblical concept.

Overall, these figures still show the esteem that Christ has in popular culture, with less than a fifth (19%) rejecting the notion that he is the Son of God. These figures also show a widespread belief that human beings can expect something more than life upon this earth, with only 18% rejecting the idea of life after death.

12   Supernatural

Introduction

This chapter is focused on young people's views of the supernatural. Six statements concerned spiritual beings or a supernatural realm. Pupils responded by agreement, uncertainty or disagreement. 'I believe in the devil', 'I believe in black magic' and 'I believe it is possible to contact spirits of the dead' explored basic beliefs. The statements, 'I believe that fortune-tellers can tell the future' and 'I believe in my horoscope' dealt with daily influences which might be thought to have supernatural connections. Finally pupils were posed with two statements referring to situations in which fear of the supernatural might sometimes occur: 'I am frightened of walking through a graveyard alone' and 'I am frightened of going into a church alone'.

Overview

Spiritual beings or a supernatural realm attracted credence from the following percentage of teenagers in this order: ghosts (37%), horoscopes (35%), contacting spirits of the dead (31%), the devil (19%), fortune-tellers (19%) and black magic (18%). The reverse perspective, that is to say, the percentage of teenagers who did *not* believe in these supernatural phenomena, follows only a slightly different order: contacting spirits of the dead (37%), ghosts (34%), horoscopes (34%), fortune-tellers (51%), black magic (51%) and the devil (53%).

From this presentation of the figures it is quite clear which are the three phenomena most believed in by modern teenagers (ghosts, horoscopes and contacting the spirits of the dead) and which are somewhat less believed in (fortune-tellers, black magic and the devil).

Of the two items concerning fear, the graveyard was more frightening than the empty church. While 39% said they were afraid of walking through a graveyard alone, only

11% said the same about being in an empty church; the reverse perspective showed that 46% were not afraid of walking alone through a graveyard and 67% would not mind being alone in a church.

Table 12.1   Supernatural: overview

	Agree %	Not certain %	Disagree %
I believe in the devil	19	28	53
I believe in black magic	18	31	51
I believe it is possible to contact the spirits of the dead	31	32	37
I believe in my horoscope	35	31	34
I believe that fortune-tellers can tell the future	19	30	51
I believe in ghosts	37	29	34
I am frightened of going into a church alone	11	22	67
I am frightened of walking through a graveyard alone	39	15	46

Does gender make a difference?

The pattern of responses concerning the devil shows that more boys than girls believe in the devil and more boys than girls disbelieve in the devil. While just over a fifth of boys (21%) believe in the devil, only 17% of girls do so; conversely while 52% of girls do not believe in the devil, 54% of boys disbelieve. Consequently more girls than boys are uncertain what to think on this issue. While 25% of boys are unsure, their uncertainty is shared by 31% of girls.

This pattern is similar to that found for belief in black magic and for ghosts. Again more boys than girls believe and disbelieve. While 20% of boys believe in black magic, only 16% of girls do so and, while just under half of girls (49%) disbelieve in it, just over half of boys (53%) share their disbelief. While 38% of boys believe in ghosts, only 36% of girls do so; while 32% of girls doubt the existence of ghosts, it is 36% of boys who share their view.

Otherwise, there are three main areas of difference between the sexes. Girls are more inclined than boys to be frightened of walking alone through graveyards, to believe in their horoscopes and to believe that fortune-tellers can tell the future. Thus, while a quarter (25%) of boys are frightened of walking through a graveyard, it is more than half (53%) of girls who share this fear with them. The reverse perspective confirms this finding. Nearly twice as many boys as girls are not frightened of lonely graveyards. While 61% of boys are unafraid, the figure for girls is 32%. Nearly twice as many girls (46%) as boys (24%) believe their horoscopes and the reverse perspective underlines this by showing that, while only 23% of girls are able to reject their horoscopes, exactly double the number of boys (46%) are able to do so. Similarly, while 14% of boys believe fortune-tellers can do as they say, the corresponding figure for girls is significantly higher at 24%; and, while three out of five boys (61%) think that the claims of fortune-tellers are untrue, it is only two out of five (41%) girls who share this opinion.

Table 12.2 Supernatural: by gender

	Male %	Female %
I believe in the devil	21	17
I believe in black magic	20	16
I believe it is possible to contact the spirits of the dead	30	33
I believe in my horoscope	24	46
I believe that fortune-tellers can tell the future	14	24
I believe in ghosts	38	36
I am frightened of going into a church alone	11	11
I am frightened of walking through a graveyard alone	25	53

The remaining items show differences of no more than 4% between the sexes, with one exception. The number of boys (30%) who believe it is possible to contact the spirits of the dead is similar to the number of girls (33%), but the number of boys who rule this possibility out completely is considerably higher (41%) compared with 32% of girls. In this matter, then, boys show more cynicism. As a result the number of uncertain girls is higher than the number of uncertain boys (35% against 29%).

Indeed, girls consistently show themselves to be more uncertain than boys on these issues (apart from going into a church alone, where 22% of boys are uncertain against 21% of girls).

Does age make a difference?

The shift between years nine and ten shows a consistent, but small, movement towards belief in the supernatural. For example, while 18% of year nine pupils believe in the devil, 20% of year ten pupils do so; while 16% of year nine pupils believe in black magic, 20% do so a year later; while 30% of year nine pupils believe it is possible to contact the spirits of the dead, this figure rises by 3% in the year; while 34% of year nine pupils believe in their horoscopes, 37% do so in year ten; while 18% of year nine pupils believe fortune-tellers can tell the future, 20% do so in year ten. Only the number of pupils believing in ghosts (which was high already) remains constant at 37%.

Table 12.3   Supernatural: by age

	Year 9 %	Year 10 %
I believe in the devil	18	20
I believe in black magic	16	20
I believe it is possible to contact the spirits of the dead	30	33
I believe in my horoscope	34	37
I believe that fortune-tellers can tell the future	18	20
I believe in ghosts	37	37
I am frightened of going into a church	12	10
I am frightened of walking through a graveyard alone	41	38

The reverse perspective confirms this movement towards belief in the supernatural. Thus, while 55% of pupils do not believe in the devil in year nine, only 51% hold this opinion in year ten; while 53% of pupils reject black magic in year nine, 49% do so in year ten; while 37% of pupils reject the possibility of contacting the spirits of the dead in year nine, this figure falls by 1% a year later; while 34% of pupils do not believe in their horoscopes in year nine, this figure for year ten is 33%; while 52% of pupils dismiss fortune-tellers in year nine, only 49% do so in year ten; even the number of pupils rejecting belief in ghosts drops by 1% in the same period from 34% to 33%.

The two items dealing with fear show a drop over the year. Over two out of five (41%) pupils in year nine are frightened of walking alone through graveyards, but this falls to 38% in year ten, and the number of pupils who are not frightened of lonely graveyards rises from 44% in year nine to 48% in year ten. In the same way, the number of pupils frightened of going into a church alone drops from 12% in year nine to 10% in year ten, and the reverse perspective shows that, while 66% of pupils are not frightened in year nine, 69% of pupils are without fear a year later.

Does church attendance make a difference?

We now split the teenagers into three groups: those who attend church weekly, those who attend church occasionally and those who never attend church, and we make a comparison of their ideas about the supernatural.

The weekly churchgoers are, in the main, different from the other two groups. For example, 34% of weekly churchgoers believe in the devil, as against 18% of occasional and 17% of non-churchgoers; 12% of weekly churchgoers believe in black magic as against 17% of occasional churchgoers and 19% of non-churchgoers; 23% of weekly churchgoers believe it is possible to contact spirits of the dead, as against 32% of the other two groups; 23% of weekly churchgoers believe their horoscopes, while the figure for occasional churchgoers stands at 38% and for non-attenders at 36%. Only just over one in ten (12%) of weekly churchgoers believe that fortune-tellers can tell the future, but a fifth (20%) of occasional churchgoers and non-attenders believe this. Belief in ghosts is not quite so marked, but is in the same direction. While 31% of weekly churchgoers believe in ghosts, the figure for occasional churchgoers is 39% and for non-attenders is 36%.

Table 12.4   Supernatural: by church attendance

	Weekly %	Sometimes %	Never %
I believe in the devil	34	18	17
I believe in black magic	12	17	19
I believe it is possible to contact the spirits of the dead	23	32	32
I believe in my horoscope	23	38	36
I believe that fortune-tellers can tell the future	12	20	20
I believe in ghosts	31	39	36
I am frightened of going into a church alone	6	12	11
I am frightened of walking through a graveyard alone	39	41	38

The comparison between the three groups in their fear of walking alone through a graveyard is less distinct and we discuss this, and the figures about the devil, at the end of this chapter. While 39% of weekly churchgoers express fear of churchyards, the figure for occasional churchgoers is 41% and for non-churchgoers is 38%. Fear of a lonely church is differently felt. Only 6% of weekly churchgoers would be afraid of an empty church building, as compared with 12% of occasional churchgoers and 11% of non-churchgoers.

This distinction between the groups is substantially confirmed by the reverse perspective, though a cluster of items shows an interesting tendency among occasional churchgoers. So far as disbelief in the devil is concerned, 45% of weekly churchgoers contrast with 51% of occasional churchgoers and 56% of non-churchgoers. Black magic shows the same sort of weighting. While 65% of weekly churchgoers disbelieve in black magic, it is 50% of the other two groups who are similarly sceptical. Weekly churchgoers are also much more inclined to disbelieve in contacting the spirits of the dead, horoscopes, fortune-tellers and ghosts.

So, 46% of weekly churchgoers disbelieve in the possibility of contacting departed spirits, as against 32% of occasional churchgoers and 38% of non-churchgoers; 49% of weekly churchgoers disbelieve in horoscopes, as against 30% of occasional churchgoers and 34% of non-churchgoers; 64% of weekly churchgoers are dismissive of fortune-tellers, as against 46% of occasional churchgoers and 51% of non-churchgoers; and 41% of weekly churchgoers do not believe in ghosts, as against 30% of occasional churchgoers and 35% of non-churchgoers.

What we comment on at the end of the chapter is the relatively low percentage of occasional churchgoers who reject contacting spirits of the dead, horoscopes, fortune-tellers and ghosts.

The reverse perspective on the items on fear shows that fear of graveyards is only slightly connected with church attendance. While 44% of weekly churchgoers and 43% of occasional churchgoers are unafraid, it is 49% of non-churchgoers who feel the same way. Weekly churchgoers are much more likely not to be afraid of being alone in a church (85%) as compared with occasional churchgoers (68%) and non-churchgoers (64%).

Does belief in God make a difference?

We now look in detail at those who do not attend a church and explore differences in the opinions of three distinct groups: 'theists', 'agnostics' and 'atheists' (see page 7).

The statistics show that theists are much more likely to be supernaturalists than are the others. Theists are more likely than the other groups of teenagers to believe in the devil, to believe it is possible to contact the spirits of the dead, to trust their horoscopes, to accept the predictions of fortune-tellers, to believe in ghosts and to be frightened of being alone in a graveyard or church. Although these findings are consistent, what is more surprising is that atheists in significant numbers also believe in the supernatural and, on some issues, atheists are more inclined to believe than are agnostics.

Table 12.5   Supernatural: by belief among non-churchgoers

	Theist %	Agnostic %	Atheist %
I believe in the devil	26	10	19
I believe in black magic	21	17	21
I believe it is possible to contact the spirits of the dead	41	29	30
I believe in my horoscope	45	37	30
I believe that fortune-tellers can tell the future	28	19	15
I believe in ghosts	46	34	34
I am frightened of going into a church alone	14	10	10
I am frightened of walking through a graveyard alone	48	41	29

For example, while more than a quarter of theists (26%) believe in the devil, 19% of atheists also believe; yet only 10% of agnostics share this conviction. Similarly, while 21% of both theists and atheists believe in black magic, only 17% of agnostics do so. With regard to black magic the finding is confirmed by the reverse perspective: 45% of agnostics do not believe in it as compared with 49% of theists and 55% of atheists. With regard to disbelief in the devil, 48% of theists, 50% of agnostics and 65% of atheists disbelieve.

The other figures, both from the point of view of belief and disbelief, are very consistent. While 30% of atheists believe in their horoscopes, 37% of agnostics and 45% of theists do so; while 15% of atheists believe in fortune-tellers, 19% of agnostics and 28% of theists do so; while 34% of atheists and agnostics believe in ghosts, 46% of theists do so; while 29% of agnostics and 30% of atheists believe it is possible to contact the spirits of the dead, 41% of theists do so.

The reverse perspective demonstrates the same overall pattern. Theists believe in the supernatural most, atheists believe least and agnostics are most uncertain. While 27% of theists and 33% of agnostics reject the possibility of contacting spirits of the dead, it is nearly half (49%) of atheists who do so; while a quarter of theists (26%) and agnostics (27%) reject their horoscopes, it is 44% of atheists who do so; while 41% of theists and 46% of agnostics reject fortune-tellers, it is 62% of atheists who do so; while 26% of theists doubt the existence of ghosts, it is 30% of agnostics and 44% of atheists who do so.

On every single item the agnostics show themselves to be the most uncertain of the three groups. Two out of five (40%) agnostics are unsure about the existence of the devil, 38% are unsure about black magic and contacting spirits of the dead and 36% are not sure of their horoscopes and ghosts. Atheists are least uncertain and theists somewhere in between. Thus, 16% of atheists are unsure about the devil, compared with 26% of theists; 24% of atheists are unsure about black magic, compared with 30% of theists; 21% of atheists cannot make up their minds about contacting spirits of the dead, compared with 32% of theists; 26% of atheists are unsure about horoscopes, compared with 29% of theists; and 22% of atheists are not sure about ghosts, compared with 28% of theists.

With regard to fear, 59% of agnostics would not be frightened of going in to a church by themselves, nor would 62% of theists or 69% of atheists. It is the graveyard which is least frightening to the atheists. A smaller number of atheists would be frightened (29%) than is the case with agnostics (41%) and theists (48%) and a larger number of atheists would not be frightened (60%), as compared with 39% of theists and 44% of agnostics.

Does denomination make a difference?

The previous section looked at those who never attend church. This section examines those who attend weekly, either in an Anglican, Free Church or Roman Catholic setting.

The Free Church young people stand a little apart from the Anglicans and the Roman Catholics. The Free Church young people are more inclined than the other two groups to believe in the devil and to reject horoscopes, ghosts, contacting the spirits of the dead and fortune-tellers. Thus, while 40% of Free Church young people believe in the devil, only 27% of Anglican and 31% of Roman Catholic young people do so. Conversely, 43% of Free Church young people disbelieve in the devil, while 44% of Roman Catholic and 48% of Anglican teenagers think the same way. Only 18% of Free Church young people believe in their horoscopes, compared with 23% of Anglicans and 29% of Roman Catholics. From the perspective of disbelief, well over half (57%) of Free Church young people reject the practice of horoscopes, but the figure for Anglicans (48%) and Roman Catholics (37%) is under half. Likewise, 24% of Free Church teenagers believe in ghosts, as against 30% of Anglicans and 39% of Roman Catholics; conversely, half (50%) of Free Church young people scorn belief in ghosts, as against 39% of Anglicans and 32% of Roman Catholics.

Table 12.6   Supernatural: by denomination

	Catholic %	Anglican %	Free %
I believe in the devil	31	27	40
I believe in black magic	11	10	10
I believe it is possible to contact the spirits of the dead	26	22	20
I believe in my horoscope	29	23	18
I believe that fortune-tellers can tell the future	12	11	10
I believe in ghosts	39	30	24
I am frightened of going into a church alone	5	5	5
I am frightened of walking through a graveyard alone	44	37	39

The other items are more similar in the percentages which believe but dissimilar in the percentages which disbelieve. So, 20% of Free Church, 22% of Anglican and 26% of Roman Catholic young people believe it is possible to contact the spirits of the dead, but there is a 10% gap between the young people on the matter of disbelief. While 52% of Free Church young people reject the possibility of departed spirits, it is 42% of both Anglicans and Roman Catholics who do so. In the same way, 10% of Free Church, 11% of Anglican and 12% of Roman Catholic young people believe in fortune-tellers, but the numbers who disbelieve are rather different. Nearly three quarters (73%) of Free Church young people reject fortune-tellers, as compared with 62% of Anglicans and 59% of Roman Catholics.

What this analysis shows is that, while Free Church young people are more predisposed to disbelieve in many supernaturally linked practices, the Roman Catholic teenagers are less distinct from the general non-churchgoing population, as we shall see later.

Fear of going into a church alone is almost identical. While 5% of all groups would be frightened of this, 88% of both Free Church and Roman Catholic young people and 87% of Anglican young people would not be frightened. Fear of being alone in a graveyard is to be found among 37% of Anglican, 39% of Free Church and 44% of Roman Catholic young people, and the reverse perspective shows percentages of 46%, 42% and 41% respectively.

Implications

A considerable minority of young people believes in the supernatural. In saying this, it is clear that in some cases the idea of belief implies *trust* and in others it implies an *acknowledgement of existence*. Far more young people who attend church weekly believe in the devil than is the case in the sample as a whole. By believing in the devil churchgoing young people mean that they believe in the reality and existence of evil, even personal and supernatural evil. Considerably far fewer young people who attend church weekly believe in horoscopes than is the case in the sample as a whole, and here the churchgoers must mean that they do not accept the validity of horoscopes, they do not trust them. The existence of horoscopes is not a matter of dispute.

Weekly churchgoers are sceptical about fortune-tellers and black magic. Their Christian beliefs are contrary to a stream of western culture at this point. In essence, though, the figures imply that there are two streams, a popular supernaturalist or semi-supernaturalist stream and a cynical, unbelieving, non-supernaturalist stream which rejects the whole package of horoscopes, ghosts, seances and fortune-telling. The figures on horoscopes, for example, show that approximately a third of young people believe in them, a third are not sure and a third reject them. The same sort of balance applies to attempts to contact spirits of the dead and ghosts. Atheists tend to follow the non-supernaturalist stream and girls in far larger numbers than boys follow the supernaturalist stream.

These generalisations allow exceptions, but the difference between girls and boys is very marked: nearly twice as many girls as boys believe in horoscopes and more than one and a half times as many girls as boys believe in fortune-tellers. Atheists, who are more likely to be male in a ratio of about three to two, show scepticism about fortune-tellers, seances and horoscopes. Thus, despite the scientific and technological basis of culture, there is evidence of beliefs in practices with a supernatural connection. At the same time, there is a strong acceptance of testing, measurement, science and rationalism. In other words this is a scientific age with New Age overtones, and this jumble of concepts is discernible in the figures presented in this chapter.

Weekly churchgoers, as we have said, tend to reject horoscopes and fortune-tellers more vigorously than do their non-churchgoing contemporaries, but this is not true for occasional churchgoers. Occasional churchgoers are actually *less* likely to reject the possibility of contacting spirits of the dead, horoscopes, fortune-tellers and ghosts than do non-churchgoers or weekly churchgoers. This may tell us something about the personalities of occasional churchgoers or about their weaker grasp of Christian doctrine. Occasional churchgoers are most frightened of going alone into a church and of walking alone through a graveyard. Whether, therefore, the slightly greater proneness to fear among occasional churchgoers leads to their predisposition to rely on horoscopes and fortune-tellers can only be checked by further research.

The figures on walking alone through a graveyard suggest that there may be natural explanations for this fear. For instance, girls in the 13 to 15 year old age group might be frightened of being molested or attacked in a lonely place. This would explain why more than twice as many girls as boys are frightened of being alone in graveyards while exactly the same numbers of girls as boys are frightened of being alone in a church. This would also explain why fear of being alone in a graveyard goes down between years nine and ten while the items dealing with seances, horoscopes and fortune-tellers increase.

Non-churchgoing theists have been shown in previous chapters to have a moral outlook akin to that of church-goers. They tend to be law-abiding. On the matter of seances, horoscopes and fortune-tellers, however, theists, because of their predilections for these activities, are noticeably distinct from weekly churchgoers. This difference shows, therefore, one of the effects of regular church-going. It provides a doctrinal basis by which supernaturalistic or semi-supernaturalistic activities can be evaluated. So far as approach of the churches to young people is concerned, it is apparent that the supernatural elements of Christianity are likely to be attractive or comprehensible to those teenagers who already feel that this is the sort of world they live in. In other words, while atheists may be attracted by the rationality of Christianity, non-churchgoing theists and other supernaturalists may be attracted by the supernaturalism of Christianity.

13 Worries

Introduction

This chapter explores young people's worries by presenting them with six statements, each beginning with the words, 'I am worried about...'. The topics covered by the statements concerned getting AIDS, being attacked by pupils from other schools, going out alone at night in the local area, getting on with other people, attractiveness to the opposite sex and one's own sex life. To each statement the young people responded by agreeing, disagreeing or expressing uncertainty.

Overview

Young people are most worried about getting AIDS and least worried about being attacked by pupils from other schools. Arranging their worries from greatest to least, the figures show that 62% worry about getting AIDS, 50% about getting on with other people, 32% about their attractiveness to the opposite sex, 29% about going out in the local area at night, 17% about their sex lives and 15% about being attacked by pupils from other schools.

Table 13.1   Worries: overview

	Agree %	Not certain %	Disagree %
I am worried about:			
my sex life	17	24	59
how I get on with other people	50	23	27
my attractiveness to the opposite sex	32	24	44
getting AIDS	62	17	21
going out alone at night in my area	29	16	55
being attacked by pupils from other schools	15	22	63

The reverse perspective confirms this order. Only 21% are not worried about getting AIDS and 27% about how they get on with other people. Otherwise 44% are not worried about their attractiveness to the opposite sex, 55% about going out into their local areas at night and 63% about being attacked by pupils from other schools.

Less than a quarter of pupils are uncertain about their worries. The least uncertain matter concerns going out alone at night in the local area (16%) and the most concerns attractiveness to the opposite sex (24%).

Does gender make a difference?

On three matters there are considerable differences between males and females. A mere 15% of boys are worried about going out alone at night in their area, compared with 43% of girls; put the other way, 71% of boys do not worry about going out alone at night, but only 40% of girls are free of worry in this respect. More girls (35%) also worry about their attractiveness to the opposite sex than do boys (28%) and fewer girls (40%) are free of this sort of worry than are boys (49%). In general girls are more inclined than boys to worry how they get on with other people. More than half of the girls (54%), compared with just under half of the boys (47%), are worried about this and, again, fewer girls (24%) are free of this worry than are boys (30%).

Table 13.2 Worries: by gender

	Male %	Female %
I am worried about:		
my sex life	16	18
how I get on with other people	47	54
my attractiveness to the opposite sex	28	35
getting AIDS	62	61
going out alone at night in my area	15	43
being attacked by pupils from other schools	15	15

The only issue on which girls and boys showed an almost identical level of worry referred to the possibility of catching AIDS; 62% of boys and 61% of girls were worried by this, and 22% of boys and 21% of girls were free of this worry.

The greater tendency of girls to worry, however, was found in the percentages of each sex which claimed to be unconcerned on a particular matter. Thus, while 16% of boys were worried about their sex lives, as compared with 18% of girls, it was far more boys (64%) than girls (54%) who were free of this worry. In the same way, while the same percentage of boys and girls (15%) were worried about being attacked by pupils from other schools, it was slightly more boys (64%) who were free of this worry than girls (61%).

On all the issues except getting on with other people (on which the difference was only 1%) more girls showed uncertainty than boys. The greatest divergence was on the matter of their sex lives: 28% of girls were not sure whether they were worried about this, compared with 20% of boys.

Does age make a difference?

The trend showed worries to decrease slightly with age, apart from the worry about AIDS. While 17% of year nine pupils are worried about their sex lives, it is 16% of year ten pupils who feel this way; conversely while 57% of year nine pupils are not worried about their sex lives, 61% of year ten pupils are unworried about this. While 32% of year nine and year ten pupils are worried about their attractiveness to the opposite sex, it is 43% of year nine pupils and 45% of year ten pupils who are free of worry on this issue. While 31% of year nine pupils are worried about going out alone at night in their area, fewer (28%) year ten pupils feel this way; conversely it is 52% of year nine pupils and 57% of year ten pupils who have no worries on this matter. Worry about getting on with other people remains completely static over the year.

Worry about AIDS shows a 1% shift towards greater concern, a finding confirmed by both perspectives. While 61% of year nine pupils are worried about catching AIDS, this figure has risen to 62% a year later and the percentage free of this worry drops by 1% in the same period: 22% of pupils are not worried in year nine, compared with 21% of pupils in year ten.

Table 13.3   Worries: by age

	Year 9 %	Year 10 %
I am worried about:		
my sex life	17	16
how I get on with other people	50	50
my attractiveness to the opposite sex	32	32
getting AIDS	61	62
going out alone at night in my area	31	28
being attacked by pupils from other schools	16	14

The percentage of uncertain pupils changes between years nine and ten by no more than four percentage points on any item.

Does church attendance make a difference?

This section examines pupils' worries in the light of their church attendance and makes comparison between three distinct groups: those who never attend church, those who attend church sometimes and those who attend church nearly every week.

Table 13.4   Worries: by church attendance

	Weekly %	Sometimes %	Never %
I am worried about:			
my sex life	18	18	15
how I get on with other people	56	55	46
my attractiveness to the opposite sex	37	35	29
getting AIDS	58	63	62
going out alone at night in my area	38	33	25
being attacked by pupils from other schools	17	16	14

Both weekly churchgoers and non-churchgoers are most worried by AIDS and least worried about being attacked by pupils from other schools, and the severity of the other worries is ranged between these two extremes in almost the same order by weekly churchgoers and non-churchgoers. In this sense the difference between churchgoers and non-churchgoers is fundamentally in the percentages who are worried on particular issues rather than in the rank ordering of things that worry them.

A smaller percentage of weekly churchgoers (58%) than non-churchgoers (62%) is worried about contracting AIDS, and this finding is confirmed by the reverse perspective because 21% of non-churchgoers are unworried about AIDS compared with 25% of weekly churchgoers.

On all the other issues weekly churchgoers are *more* worried than non-churchgoers. Whereas 56% of weekly churchgoers are worried about how they get on with other people, it is 46% of non-churchgoers who worry in this way; whereas 38% of weekly churchgoers are worried about going out at night alone, it is 25% of non-churchgoers who share this matter; whereas 37% of weekly churchgoers worry about how they get on with the opposite sex, it is 29% of non-churchgoers who are worried on this count; whereas 18% of weekly churchgoers are worried about their sex lives, it is 15% of non-churchgoers who share this concern; whereas 17% of weekly churchgoers are worried about being attacked by pupils from other schools, it is 14% of non-churchgoers who are anxious on this matter.

The reverse perspective confirms this picture in the sense that more weekly churchgoers worry than non-churchgoers. The main difference arises in the order of the various worries. More non-churchgoers worry about AIDS than they do about how they get on with other people, but more weekly churchgoers worry about how they get on with other people than they do about AIDS. The percentages give the detail. Whereas 25% of weekly churchgoers are not worried that they will catch AIDS, it is 21% of non-churchgoers who are free of this worry. On the other hand, whereas 21% of weekly churchgoers are unworried about how they get on with other people, it is 31% of non-churchgoers who are similarly confident; whereas 38% of weekly churchgoers are free of worry about their attractiveness to the opposite sex, it is 48% of non-churchgoers who are in the same fortunate position; whereas 44% of weekly churchgoers are not worried about going out to their area alone at night, it is 60% of non-churchgoers who have no worry on these lines; whereas 58% of weekly churchgoers are not worried about being attacked by pupils from other schools, the corresponding figure for non-churchgoers is 65%.

Occasional churchgoers are intermediate between weekly churchgoers and non-churchgoers, except on the issue of getting AIDS. Occasional churchgoers (63%) are slightly more worried about getting AIDS than are the other two groups, whichever perspective is used. Only 20% of occasional churchgoers have no worries about AIDS, compared with 21% of non-churchgoers and 25% of weekly churchgoers.

Does belief in God make a difference?

This section examines those who do not attend church and explores the differences in the worries of the three distinct groups: 'theists', 'agnostics' and 'atheists' (see page 7).

Table 13.5   Worries: by belief among non-churchgoers

	Theist %	Agnostic %	Atheist %
I am worried about:			
my sex life	17	15	15
how I get on with other people	51	47	42
my attractiveness to the opposite sex	30	29	27
getting AIDS	66	62	59
going out alone at night in my area	31	28	20
being attacked by pupils from other schools	19	14	12

On each of the items more theists are worried than agnostics and more agnostics are worried than atheists. When the reverse perspective is employed, agnostics emerge on four items as slightly more worried than theists. Quite clearly atheists in greater numbers report themselves to be unworried on all the issues, while agnostics report themselves in greater numbers to be uncertain about how to interpret their feelings.

Thus, 66% of theists, 62% of agnostics and 59% of atheists are worried about getting AIDS and these contrast with 19% of agnostics, 20% of theists and 24% of atheists who are not worried about getting AIDS. Similarly, 51% of theists, 47% of agnostics and 42% of atheists are worried about how they get on with other people, while 28% of agnostics, 31% of theists and 34% of atheists are free of this sort of worry. In the same way, 30% of theists, 29% of agnostics and 27% of atheists are worried about their attractiveness to the opposite sex, while 45% of agnostics, 48% of theists and 52% of atheists have no anxieties on this matter. In fact, 17% of theists and 15% of both agnostics and atheists are worried about their sex lives, while 59% of agnostics, 60% of theists and 66% of atheists do not find this a cause for concern.

Theists report themselves to be more concerned than the other groups on the issues of going out alone at night and being attacked by pupils from other schools, and this concern is found in both perspectives. There are 31% of theists, 28% of agnostics and 20% of atheists who are worried about going out alone at night and 54%, 55% and 68% respectively of theists, agnostics and atheists who are unworried. Likewise, there are 19% of theists, 14% of agnostics and 12% of atheists who are concerned about being attacked by pupils from other schools and 61%, 62% and 69% respectively of these groups who are unconcerned.

Does denomination make a difference?

The previous section looked at young people who never attend church. This section examines those who attend weekly, either in an Anglican, Free Church or Roman Catholic setting.

The figures show no clear pattern. On some issues young churchgoers from one denomination are more likely to be worried, while on other issues it is young churchgoers from other denominations. For example, it is true that more

Roman Catholic (23%) young people fear attack by pupils from other schools than is the case with Anglican (14%) and Free Church (15%) young people. This finding is confirmed by the reverse perspective: while 56% of Roman Catholics are not worried about attacks by pupils from other schools, it is 58% of Free Church young people and 60% of Anglicans who have no such concern. It is also true that Anglicans seem to be the most socially assured of the young people. While 60% of Roman Catholic and Free Church young people are worried about how they get on with others, it is only 54% of Anglicans who have this worry, and the number of Anglicans with no concern about their ability to get on with others is the highest (22%), compared with 17% of Free Church young people and 18% of Roman Catholics. Slightly more Free Church young people are worried about their attractiveness to the opposite sex (40%) than is the case with Anglicans (38%) and Roman Catholics (37%), and this worry is confirmed by the reverse perspective because 34% of Free Church young people are confident of their attractiveness to the opposite sex, compared with 35% of Anglicans and 40% of Roman Catholics.

Table 13.6   Worries: by denomination

	Catholic %	Anglican %	Free %
I am worried about:			
my sex life	19	17	17
how I get on with other people	60	54	60
my attractiveness to the opposite sex	37	38	40
getting AIDS	62	58	55
going out alone at night in my area	37	41	40
being attacked by pupils from other schools	23	14	15

On the major issue of AIDS, 62% of Roman Catholics are worried that they will catch it, compared with fewer Anglicans (58%) and even fewer Free Church young people (55%). The percentage of those in each denomination with no worries about catching AIDS is almost exactly the same:

23% of both Anglicans and Roman Catholics and 24% of Free Church young people.

Roman Catholics are least worried about going out alone at night (37%), compared with 40% of Free Church young people and 41% of Anglicans; on the other hand 46% of Roman Catholics are not frightened of their local area and this compares with 40% of Anglican and 38% of Free Church young people.

Implications

The most serious worry young people have is of contracting AIDS and, since sexual activity is on the agenda of many of these young people, this is a realistic worry. Health education programmes and television advertising have clearly raised young people's awareness of AIDS. Yet, approximately a fifth (21%) of young people is not worried. The most obvious explanation for the lack of worry expressed by this minority is either that they intend to practise safe sex or that they intend to abstain from intercourse. In favour of the latter explanation is the slight but noticeable increase in the percentage of weekly churchgoers (25%) who do not fear AIDS. Moreover, whereas more females than males attend church weekly, male and female fear of AIDS is almost identical. The different levels of concern about catching AIDS between weekly churchgoers and non-churchgoers cannot therefore be due to gender differences in attendance rates.

Well-publicised attacks on young women at night may contribute to a fear by more than two out of five girls (43%) of going out alone at night. These are astonishing figures to find in a civilised society, particularly in view of the smaller percentage of women (40%) with no worries on this matter; more girls are frightened of going out alone than the number of those who are not frightened of going out alone. Even 15% of boys fear going out alone and, when it is remembered that this survey covers young people in their mid-teens, the perception of crime in British streets is sharpened. It is not solely a fear of rape or sexual crime against women, nor is it the kind of fear which might be found among little children whose imaginations have been shaped by fairy stories, but instead it is a general and realistic fear of crime against the person. The hopeful sign is that this fear declines slightly between years nine and ten.

This fear of going out alone at night has its daytime counterpart. The same number of boys as is frightened of going out alone at night is frightened of being attacked by pupils from other schools. However, the situations at night and day are not quite the same because more boys are confident about going out at night (71%) than are unworried by attack from pupils from another school (64%). But the possibility of inter-school violence is a real one in the minds of nearly a third of pupils, and this fear applies to both sexes (only 61% of girls are *not* worried about attack by another school). There is surely a case here for senior staff from schools within the same neighbourhood or on similar bus routes to take effective joint action to reduce the fear uncovered by this survey. The figures unmistakably demonstrate that fear of attack by pupils from other schools is greatest among Roman Catholics (who may well be attending voluntary aided schools). The data suggest that there should be much close co-operation between denominational and county schools to eradicate this fear. It is unacceptable that such a large number of pupils should have to live with these unnecessary worries. Indeed, the low opinion which many pupils have of teachers (see chapter 3, *School*) may stem partly from their perception of the ineffectiveness of staff in coping with these real problems.

Half of these young people are worried about how they get on with others. They are not socially confident, partly, perhaps, because they are worried about their attractiveness to the opposite sex. The figures show that boys are both less worried about their attractiveness to the opposite sex and less worried about how they get on with other people. They are also less worried about their sex lives. Yet the worried group of young people contrasts with a self-assured minority of young people who feel attractive to the opposite sex and think they can easily mix with others. The group dynamics of young people's gatherings is suggested by the detail of the figures: 30% of boys and 24% of girls feel they can interact socially without difficulty. Overlapping with the socially confident group is a bigger group of 49% of boys and 40% of girls who are confident about their sexual attractiveness. By subtracting the relevant sets of figures the implication is that there are 19% of boys and 16% of girls who believe they are sexually attractive but who lack the social confidence to express it. The scope for pain and romance is considerable and well exploited by teenage music, but it is also an area which clergy, teachers, parents and counsellors should thoroughly understand.

14 Work

Introduction

This chapter explores young people's ideas about work, unemployment and Youth Training Schemes. Three statements concerned work alone. These were: 'I think it is important to work hard when I get a job', 'A job gives you a sense of purpose' and 'I want to get to the top in my work when I get a job'. Two statements concerned YTS: 'Youth Training Schemes (YTS) teach young people useful skills' and 'I would rather be unemployed on social security than join the Youth Training Scheme (YTS)'. The Youth Training Schemes have been replaced by Training Credit Schemes, but the wording of the questionnaire was drafted before this change was made. In concept the two schemes are similar and so the contrasts which are drawn between training schemes and unemployment are still valid. Three statements concerned unemployment: 'I would not like to be unemployed', 'I would rather be unemployed on social security than get a job I don't like doing' and 'Most unemployed people could have a job if they really wanted to'.

Overview

Young people are overwhelmingly convinced of the need to work hard when they get a job (94%) and most are ambitious to get to the top (86%). More than three quarters (77%) agree that a job gives a sense of purpose; 19% are not sure about this and 4% disagree.

Youth Training Schemes are viewed as providing useful skills by more than two-thirds of young people (67%). However, 10% of young people disagree with this positive assessment and 23% are uncertain. The negative assessment of youth training is underlined by 9% of young people who would rather be unemployed on social security than take part in a YTS. Nevertheless the vast majority (64%) of young people take the opposite view and would prefer a YTS placement. Just over a quarter (27%) are uncertain which option they would prefer.

Table 14.1   Work: overview

	Agree %	Not certain %	Disagree %
I think it is important to work hard when I get a job	94	4	2
A job gives you a sense of purpose	77	19	4
I want to get to the top in my work when I get a job	86	11	3
I would rather be unemployed on social security than get a job I don't like doing	18	24	58
I would not like to be unemployed	86	5	9
Youth Training Schemes (YTS) teach young people useful skills	67	23	10
I would rather be unemployed on social security than join the Youth Training Scheme (YTS)	9	27	64
Most unemployed people could have a job if they really wanted to	56	24	20

A huge majority of young people (86%) would not like to be unemployed, but there is a dissident minority (9%) who would not mind, and a small group of 5% who are uncertain on the matter. A rather larger group (18%) would prefer unemployment to a job they did not enjoy, but the majority (58%) would settle for an uncongenial job rather than drawing social security. A quarter of young people (24%) cannot make up their minds which of these possibilities they prefer.

Sympathy for unemployed people is in short supply. More than half of young people (56%) think that most unemployed people could get a job if they really wanted and only 20% of the teenagers disagree with this; 24% are uncertain.

Does gender make a difference?

Gender differences over ideas about work are small. Slightly more girls (95%) than boys (93%) think it is important to work hard when they get a job and slightly more boys (79%) than girls (75%) think that a job gives a sense of purpose. Boys (89%) are slightly more ambitious to get to the top in their work when they get a job than are girls (84%).

Table 14.2   Work: by gender

	Male %	Female %
I think it is important to work hard when I get a job	93	95
A job gives you a sense of purpose	79	75
I want to get to the top in my work when I get a job	89	84
I would rather be unemployed on social security than get a job I don't like doing	20	16
I would not like to be unemployed	85	87
Youth Training Schemes (YTS) teach young people useful skills	68	66
I would rather be unemployed on social security than join the Youth Training Scheme (YTS)	11	8
Most unemployed people could have a job if they really wanted to	60	52

Boys are both more positive and more negative about YTS. While 68% of boys, compared with 66% of girls, think they would gain useful skills on a YTS, 12% of boys, compared with 8% of girls, disagree with this. Slightly more boys (11%) than girls (8%) would rather be unemployed on social security than join a YTS, but the percentage of boys and girls who take the opposite view is the same and amounts to nearly two-thirds (64%).

Slightly more girls (87%) than boys (85%) would not like to be unemployed, a finding confirmed by the reverse perspective which shows that 10% of boys would not mind unemployment, compared with 7% of girls. In the same vein 20% of boys, compared with 16% of girls, would prefer unemployment to a job they did not like, though it is 58% of both sexes which would make the opposite choice.

Where boys and girls do tend to take a different view is over the possibility of obtaining work. As many as 60% of boys, compared with 52% of girls, think that most unemployed people could get a job if they really wanted, and this tendency is confirmed by the 18% of boys and 22% of girls who disagree with this assessment of the economic situation.

Does age make a difference?

The main shifts shown by the age trend concern disaffection with YTS and a growing realisation by young people that they may have to do jobs they do not enjoy.

Table 14.3   Work: by age

	Year 9 %	Year 10 %
I think it is important to work hard when I get a job	95	93
A job gives you a sense of purpose	77	77
I want to get to the top in my work when I get a job	87	86
I would rather be unemployed on social security than get a job I don't like doing	19	16
I would not like to be unemployed	86	86
Youth Training Schemes (YTS) teach young people useful skills	69	64
I would rather be unemployed on social security than join the Youth Training Scheme (YTS)	8	11
Most unemployed people could have a job if they really wanted to	57	54

In year nine it is 95% of pupils who think it is important to work hard, and in year ten it is 93% of pupils who take this view; 77% of pupils in both year nine and ten think a job gives a sense of purpose and 87% of year nine pupils and 86% of year ten pupils want to get to the top in their jobs.

The prospect of unemployment is equally unattractive (86%) in both year groups, but the choice between unemployment and YTS shows a slight preference for unemployment in year ten. In year nine 8% of pupils prefer unemployment and in year ten it is 11% of pupils; this finding is underlined by the shift between the 65% in year nine to the 63% in year ten who would opt for YTS rather than unemployment. This may be because there is a fall in the number of pupils who think that YTS skills are useful. The 69% in year nine become 64% in year ten; and, while 8% of pupils do not think YTS teach useful skills in the younger year group, it is 12% of pupils who take this view in year ten.

A dawning realism about the job market is revealed in the drop from 57% to 54% of pupils who think that most unemployed people could get a job if they really wanted. The reverse perspective points in the same direction and shows that in year nine 19% of pupils disagree with this optimism, rising to 22% of pupils in year ten. In addition, while 19% of year nine pupils would rather be unemployed on social security than doing a job they did not like, this figure has dropped by 3% in year ten. The reverse perspective shows that, while 56% of pupils in year nine would choose a job they do not like in preference to unemployment, it is a larger number (60%) who would decide this way in year ten.

Does church attendance make a difference?

This section examines pupils' attitudes towards work in the light of their church attendance and makes comparison between three groups: those who never attend church, those who attend church sometimes and those who attend church nearly every week.

Weekly and occasional churchgoers demonstrate a slightly more positive evaluation of work and YTS than do non-churchgoers. Whereas 97% of weekly churchgoers and 96% of occasional churchgoers think it is important to work hard when they get a job, it is 93% of non-churchgoers who agree with them; whereas 80% of both weekly and occasional churchgoers think that a job gives a sense of purpose, it is 74% of non-churchgoers who take this view; whereas 88% of both weekly and occasional churchgoers want to get

to the top in their job, it is 85% of non-churchgoers who
share this ambition; whereas 90% of weekly churchgoers
and 88% of occasional churchgoers would not like to be
unemployed, it is 84% of non-churchgoers who have similar
feelings. Similarly, while 17% of both weekly and occasional churchgoers would prefer to be unemployed than do
a job they did not enjoy, it is 19% of non-churchgoers who
would make this decision.

Table 14.4   Work: by church attendance

	Weekly %	Sometimes %	Never %
I think it is important to work hard when I get a job	97	96	93
A job gives you a sense of purpose	80	80	74
I want to get to the top in my work when I get a job	88	88	85
I would rather be unemployed on social security than get a job I don't like doing	17	17	19
I would not like to be unemployed	90	88	84
Youth Training Schemes (YTS) teach young people useful skills	68	68	66
I would rather be unemployed on social security than join the Youth Training Scheme (YTS)	8	8	11
Most unemployed people could have a job if they really wanted to	54	57	56

The YTS is considered to teach useful skills by 68% of
both weekly and occasional churchgoers, compared with
66% of non-churchgoers. The choice between unemployment
and YTS is made in favour of unemployment by 8% of both
weekly and occasional churchgoers and 11% of non-churchgoers. The first of these findings is confirmed by the reverse
perspective. While 11% of non-churchgoers do not think the
YTS teach useful skills, it is 8% of both weekly and
occasional churchgoers who make this assessment. On the
other hand, while 66% of occasional churchgoers would
prefer YTS to unemployment, it is 63% of the other two
groups who do so.

Slightly fewer weekly churchgoers (54%) think most unemployed people could have a job if they wanted one, compared with occasional churchgoers (57%) or non-churchgoers (56%).

Does belief in God make a difference?

We now look in detail at those who do not go to church and explore the differences in the opinions of three distinct groups: 'theists', 'agnostics' and 'atheists' (see page 7).

Table 14.5   Work: by belief among non-churchgoers

	Theist %	Agnostic %	Atheist %
I think it is important to work hard when I get a job	96	94	90
A job gives you a sense of purpose	79	75	71
I want to get to the top in my work when I get a job	88	87	81
I would rather be unemployed on social security than get a job I don't like doing	20	18	19
I would not like to be unemployed	87	85	81
Youth Training Schemes (YTS) teach young people useful skills	66	68	63
I would rather be unemployed on social security than join the Youth Training Scheme (YTS)	11	8	13
Most unemployed people could have a job if they really wanted to	57	57	55

The analysis shows that theists are slightly more positive towards work than are agnostics or atheists and that agnostics are slightly more positive towards the YTS than are the other two groups.

While 90% of atheists and 94% of agnostics think it is important to work hard when they get a job, it is 96% of theists who think this; while 71% of atheists and 75% of agnostics think that a job gives a sense of purpose, it is 79% of theists who think this; while 81% of atheists and 87% of agnostics want to get to the top when they get a job, it is 88% of theists who have this ambition; while 81% of atheists and 85% of agnostics would not like to be unemployed, it is 87% of theists who share this aversion. On the other hand, it is 68% of agnostics, compared with 66% of theists and 63% of atheists, who think that YTS teach useful skills and 8% of agnostics, compared with 11% of theists and 13% of atheists, who would choose unemployment instead of a YTS.

In each of these comparisons the atheists are clearly the group least in favour of YTS and most inclined to accept unemployment. For example, while 8% of agnostics and 10% of theists do not think YTS teach useful skills, it is 15% of atheists who make this negative evaluation; or, while 9% of theists and agnostics say they would like unemployment, it is 12% who hold this opinion.

Theists and agnostics take a slightly rosier view of the possibility of obtaining a job than do atheists. Whereas 57% of both theists and agnostics think most unemployed people could get a job if they wanted, it is 55% of atheists who think this, and it is a larger number of atheists (23%) than theists and agnostics (19% each) who disagree with this assessment.

On one matter theists, agnostics and atheists can hardly be distinguished. It is 58% of both theists and atheists and 57% of agnostics who would take a job they did not like in preference to unemployment and it is 18% of agnostics, 19% of atheists and 20% of theists who would chose unemployment in these circumstances.

Does denomination make a difference?

The previous section looked at those who never attend church. This section examines those who attend weekly, either in an Anglican, Free Church or Roman Catholic setting.

These churchgoing young people are overwhelmingly positive in their evaluation of employment. Over 96% of each group think it is important to work hard when they get a job and 91% of each group would not like to be unemployed. Nearly all these young people want to get to the top

in their job: 88% of Free Church, 87% of Anglican and 90%
of Roman Catholic teenagers express this intention.

Table 14.6   Work: by denomination

	Catholic %	Anglican %	Free %
I think it is important to work hard when I get a job	97	96	99
A job gives you a sense of purpose	81	81	80
I want to get to the top in my work when I get a job	90	87	88
I would rather be unemployed on social security than get a job I don't like doing	17	16	16
I would not like to be unemployed	91	91	91
Youth Training Schemes (YTS) teach young people useful skills	66	71	70
I would rather be unemployed on social security than join the Youth Training Scheme (YTS)	9	6	7
Most unemployed people could have a job if they really wanted to	55	50	55

The Roman Catholic young people are slightly more
critical of the YTS than are the others. Whereas 71% of
Anglican and 70% of Free Church teenagers think the YTS
teach useful skills, it is 66% of Roman Catholics who share
this opinion; and the reverse perspective shows that it is
11% of Roman Catholics, as opposed to 4% of Anglican and
6% of Free Church young people, who do not think the YTS
is useful in this way. Likewise, slightly more Roman
Catholic young people would prefer unemployment to a
YTS. While 6% of Anglican and 7% of Free Church young
people would accept unemployment instead of a YTS place,
it is 9% of Roman Catholics who would do so; and the
reverse perspective shows that, while 64% of Free Church
and 68% of Anglican young people would opt for a YTS
place rather than unemployment, it is 60% of Roman
Catholics who would do so.

There is some disagreement about the availability of work
for the unemployed. While 55% of both Roman Catholic
and Free Church young people think that most unemployed

people could find a job if they really wished, it is 50% of Anglicans who think this. The reverse perspective shows that Roman Catholics (23%) are more inclined than the other groups to see unemployment as a serious problem. In comparison it is 18% of Free Church and 19% of Anglican young people who do not think unemployed people could find a job by looking harder.

Implications

The figures presented here show that the vast majority of teenagers want to work, are determined to work hard when they get a job, are ambitious and think positively of YTS. Against this encouraging background must be set two factors. There is a small minority of approximately 10% of young people who are disillusioned and unenthusiastic about employment or the YTS; these young people have no objection to unemployment and would prefer it to a YTS. The implication is that this minority is preparing for long-term unemployment and see it as an acceptable and inevitable life-style.

The second factor which runs through these figures is naïve idealism. More than half of these young people think that unemployment is really the fault of the unemployed in the sense that, by trying harder, nearly everyone could find a job. This over-optimistic view shows signs of weakening in the shift between years nine and ten and in the growing recognition that it may be necessary to do an unpopular job instead of drawing social security. The slippage in the figures on the usefulness of YTS skills points in the same direction. However, the figures also show that it is males who agree in greater numbers than females that a job gives a sense of purpose and who think that a job can be found by all who really want one. The consequence of all this is that in those parts of England where male unemployment is especially high and where despite all their efforts the unemployed cannot secure work, some of these idealistic young people are going to find themselves deeply frustrated and disappointed.

Female attitudes to employment are very similar to those of males except in three ways. Females are slightly less ambitious to get to the top and they are slightly more inclined to take a job they do not like in preference to unemployment. They are also less convinced that a job gives a sense of purpose. Nevertheless, the differences between males and females in their approach to work are over-shadowed by the similarities and these imply that competition between males and females in many sectors of the job market will be fierce.

Churchgoers are slightly more positive about employment, hard work and YTS than are non-churchgoers. To this extent churchgoing, therefore, orientates young people towards, and not away from, the world of work. Of all the various groups examined in this analysis (boys, girls, year nine pupils, year ten pupils, non-churchgoing theists, agnostics and atheists) it is the weekly churchgoers who would least like to be unemployed and who, especially in the case of Anglican and Free Church young people, most favourably evaluate the skill training offered by the YTS.

15   Church and society

Introduction

This chapter examines the public face of religion. It is concerned with the perception which young people have of church and religion in school and society. Nine statements addressed the issues. 'Religious education should be taught in school' and 'Schools should hold a religious assembly every day' tested two important aspects of school religion. 'I want to get married in church' and 'I want my children to be baptised/christened in church' tested the value young people attached to rites of passage offered by the church. Beyond these rites the statements, 'The church seems irrelevant to life today' and 'The bible seems irrelevant to life today' explored the contemporary importance that young people attach to the teachings of the church and bible. 'Church is boring', 'I believe I can be a Christian without going to church' and 'Christian ministers/vicars/priests do a good job' concerned, among other things, reasons young people might have for non-attendance at church.

Overview

The rites of passage offered by the church receive a general endorsement from young people and there is significant support for religious education and an appreciation of Christian ministers. Otherwise, young people in large numbers think the church and the bible are irrelevant and that daily religious assemblies should definitely not be held. Many young people think church is boring.

In detail, the figures show that more than three-quarters (78%) of young people want to marry in church and well over half (57%) want their children baptised or christened in church. A third of young people (33%) think religious education should be taught in school and slightly more (36%) consider Christian ministers, vicars or priests do a good job. The reverse perspective shows the strength of these findings.

Only 5% of young people do not want to marry in church and 16% do not want their children baptised or christened. Religious education is rejected by 31% of young people (the largest group on this item, 36%, is not sure) but only 17% are critical of the work of Christian ministers (the largest group on this item, 47%, is also not sure). Daily religious assemblies in school are supported by a mere 6% of these teenagers and rejected by an overwhelming 73%.

Table 15.1   Church and Society: overview

	Agree %	Not certain %	Disagree %
Religious education should be taught in school	33	36	31
Schools should hold a religious assembly every day	6	21	73
Church is boring	51	27	22
I believe that I can be a Christian without going to church	50	33	17
I want to get married in church	78	17	5
The church seems irrelevant to life today	27	46	27
The bible seems irrelevant to life today	30	43	27
I want my children to be baptised/christened in church	57	27	16
Christian ministers/vicars/priests do a good job	36	47	17

Nearly a third of young people (30%) think the bible is irrelevant to life today and a similar number (27%) think the same thing about the church. In each case 27% of young people disagree with this damning verdict, but the largest group (46% in the case of the church and 43% in the case of the bible) cannot make up its mind. The figures also show that half (51%) of young people think church is boring; only 22% take a more positive view. Exactly half (50%) of these young people think that church attendance is unnecessary to the Christian life, an opinion disputed by 17%.

Does gender make a difference?

Girl consistently have a more favourable perception of church and religion than boys. There are six main areas where at least 10% more girls than boys demonstrate this. Whereas 50% of boys want their children baptised or christened in church, it is 64% of girls who express this wish; whereas 72% of boys want to be married in church, it is 84% of girls who agree with them; whereas 33% of boys think the church is irrelevant to life today, it is only 20% of girls who think this; whereas 36% of boys think the bible is irrelevant to life today, it is 24% of girls who take this view; whereas 27% of boys think that religious education should be taught in school, it is 38% of girls who feel the same way; and, whereas 57% of boys think that church is boring, the percentage of girls who make this judgement is 46%.

Table 15.2   Church and Society: by gender

	Male %	Female %
Religious education should be taught in school	27	38
Schools should hold a religious assembly every day	6	7
Church is boring	57	46
I believe that I can be a Christian without going to church	48	52
I want to get married in church	72	84
The church seems irrelevant to life today	33	20
The bible seems irrelevant to life today	36	24
I want my children to be baptised/christened in church	50	64
Christian ministers/vicars/priests do a good job	35	36

The reverse perspective confirms all these findings, though in each case the gender differences are less strong. Whereas 19% of boys do not want their children baptised or christened in church, it is only 13% of girls who express a similar negative wish; whereas 6% of boys do not want to be married in church, it is 4% of girls who say the same; whereas 26% of boys think the church is definitely relevant to life today, it is 29% of girls who agree with them; whereas 27% of boys think the bible is definitely relevant to life today, it is 28% of girls who take this view; whereas

39% of boys are opposed to religious education in schools, only 24% of girls agree with them; and, whereas 18% of boys do not think the church is boring, it is a quarter of girls (25%) who take this view.

As part of the pattern of gender differences, girls show themselves to be more uncertain than boys. More than half (51%) of girls cannot decide if the church is irrelevant to life today and if Christian ministers do a good job. As many as 48% of girls are not sure if the bible is irrelevant to life today. The corresponding figures for boys are 41%, 43% and 37% respectively.

The other differences between girls and boys are less pronounced. For example, it is 6% of boys and only 7% of girls who think there should be a religious assembly every day and, conversely, it is 71% of girls and 75% of boys who take the opposite view. It is 35% of boys and 36% of girls who think Christian ministers, vicars or priests do a good job and, conversely, it is 22% of boys and 13% of girls who disagree with this. It is 48% of boys and 52% of girls who believe that they can be Christians without attending church and 14% of girls and 20% of boys who think that church attendance is a necessary part of being a Christian.

Does age make a difference?

As pupils become older, they become more critical of religion and the church. This is a consistent finding illustrated by the fact that on nearly every issue year ten teenagers are less inclined than those in year nine to express uncertainty. Presumably those who were uncertain in year nine tend to become critical in year ten.

In year nine, 37% of pupils think there should be religious education at school, but this figure drops to 28% a year later; 49% think church is boring in year nine, but by year ten it is 54% who think this; 80% of year nine pupils would want to marry in church, but a year later the figure has dropped by 4%; 28% of year nine pupils think the bible seems irrelevant to life today, but a year later this figure has increased by 4%; Christian ministers, vicars or priests are thought by 38% of year nine pupils to be doing a good job, but a year later only 34% of pupils think this; 25% of year nine pupils think the church is irrelevant to life today and a year later 28% of pupils think this; 58% of pupils in year nine would want their children baptised or christened in church, but a year later only 55% of pupils have this wish; even the very small number of pupils who think schools should hold religious assemblies every day drops from 7% to 6% in year ten.

Table 15.3   Church and Society: by age

	Year 9 %	Year 10 %
Religious education should be taught in school	37	28
Schools should hold a religious assembly every day	7	6
Church is boring	49	54
I believe that I can be a Christian without going to church	50	51
I want to get married in church	80	76
The church seems irrelevant to life today	25	28
The bible seems irrelevant to life today	28	32
I want my children to be baptised/christened in church	58	55
Christian ministers/vicars/priests do a good job	38	34

The reverse perspective generally confirms this trend. The percentage of pupils who are against religious education rises from 28% to 35% over the year; the percentage of pupils who think that church is interesting falls from 23% to 20% over the year; the percentage of pupils who would not want to marry in church rises from 5% to 6%; the percentage of pupils who think the bible is irrelevant to life today remains level at 27% and the percentage of pupils who think that Christian ministers do a bad job rises from 17% to 18% over the year. The percentage of pupils who do not want their own children baptised or christened remains at 16% and the percentage against daily religious assemblies rises from 71% to 75%. One contradiction to this general trend, however, is shown by the percentage of pupils in year nine (27%) who think the church *is* relevant to modern life. A year later this figure has grown by 1%.

The issue of being a Christian without attending church is discussed at the end of this chapter. The figures hardly move between years nine and ten. There is a shift of 1% on both perspectives in favour of the view that church attendance is not a requirement for a Christian (50% of pupils take this view and 16% of pupils disagree with it in year nine).

The only issue on which pupils become more uncertain is that of religious education. While 35% of pupils in year nine cannot make up their minds, it is 37% of pupils in year ten who find themselves in this position.

Does church attendance make a difference?

When we explore the figures to see if church attendance affects perceptions of church and society, it is immediately obvious that weekly churchgoers are much more favourably disposed to school religion and the work of the church than are occasional churchgoers, and that occasional churchgoers are more favourably disposed than are non-churchgoers.

The responses to the item, 'Church is boring' illustrate the point. Whereas a fifth (20%) of weekly churchgoers agree that church is boring, it is two fifths (41%) of occasional churchgoers and nearly two thirds (65%) of non-attenders who share this opinion. Conversely, while 61% of weekly churchgoers think church is interesting, it is 25% of occasional churchgoers and 11% of non-churchgoers who make the same positive judgement.

In detail, whereas 69% of weekly churchgoers and 44% of occasional churchgoers think ministers, vicars or priests do a good job, it is only 24% of non-churchgoers who agree; whereas 82% of weekly and 69% of occasional churchgoers want to have their children baptised or christened in church, it is 43% of non-churchgoers who would wish to make use of this service; whereas 91% of weekly churchgoers and 85% of occasional churchgoers want to get married in church, it is 71% of non-churchgoers who share this desire; whereas 17% of weekly and 24% of occasional churchgoers agree that the bible is irrelevant for life today, it is 36% of non-churchgoers who hold the same opinion; whereas 61% of weekly churchgoers and 40% of occasional churchgoers think religious education should be taught in school, it is 22% of non-attenders who are supportive in this way; whereas 16% of weekly church-goers and 21% of occasional churchgoers think the church is irrelevant to modern life, it is 33% of non-churchgoers who take this view; whereas 17% of weekly and 8% of occasional churchgoers think schools should hold a daily religious assembly, it is only 3% of non-attenders who share this opinion.

Table 15.4   Church and Society: by church attendance

	Weekly %	Sometimes %	Never %
Religious education should be taught in school	61	40	22
Schools should hold a religious assembly every day	17	8	3
Church is boring	20	41	65
I believe that I can be a Christian without going to church	44	63	43
I want to get married in church	91	85	71
The church seems irrelevant to life today	16	21	33
The bible seems irrelevant to life today	17	24	36
I want my children to be baptised/christened in church	82	69	43
Christian ministers/vicars/priests do a good job	69	44	24

When teenagers are asked about whether church attend-ance is a requirement for being a Christian, the weekly churchgoers and the non-churchgoers tend to agree against the occasional churchgoers. It is 44% of weekly churchgoers and 43% of non-churchgoers who believe that it is possible to be a Christian without going to church, but the figure for occasional attenders is much higher (63%).

The opposite perspective confirms all these findings. Only 6% of weekly churchgoers and 10% of occasional churchgoers, compared with 24% of non-churchgoers, think that Christian ministers, vicars or priests do a bad job; only 4% of weekly churchgoers and 8% of occasional church-goers, compared with 24% of non-churchgoers, do not want their children baptised or christened in church; only 1% of weekly churchgoers and 3% of occasional churchgoers do not want to marry in church, compared with 7% of non-churchgoers; 53% of weekly churchgoers and 29% of occasional churchgoers think the bible is relevant for today, and this contrasts with 21% of non-churchgoers; only 10% of weekly churchgoers and 21% of occasional churchgoers think that religious education should not be taught in school, and this contrasts with 43% of non-churchgoers; 56% of weekly churchgoers and 31% of occasional churchgoers think the church is relevant for life today, but only 18% of non-churchgoers share this evaluation; and, while 51% of weekly churchgoers and 65% of occasional churchgoers think there should not be a daily religious assembly in school, it is 83% of non-churchgoers who share this conclusion.

Does belief in God make a difference?

This section focuses only on teenagers who do not attend church and explains the differences in the opinions of three distinct groups: 'theists', 'agnostics' and 'atheists' (see page 7). The figures confirm that theists are most favourable and atheists least favourable to the public face of religion.

While 64% of theists and 48% of agnostics want their children baptised or christened in church, only 28% of atheists express this wish; while 47% of theists and 61% of agnostics think church is boring, it is 80% of atheists who agree with them; while 45% of theists and 22% of agnostics think Christian ministers, vicars or priests do a good job, only 13% of atheists agree with them; while 23% of theists and 27% of agnostics think the bible is irrelevant for life today, it is more than half of the atheists (53%) who take this view; while 85% of theists and 75% of agnostics want to get married in church, it is 59% of atheists who express this wish; and, while 7% of theists and 3% of agnostics think there should be a daily religious assembly in schools, only 2% of atheists agree with them.

Table 15.5   *Church and Society: by belief among non-churchgoers*

	Theist %	Agnostic %	Atheist %
Religious education should be taught in school	39	21	12
Schools should hold a religious assembly every day	7	3	2
Church is boring	47	61	80
I believe that I can be a Christian without going to church	64	44	28
I want to get married in church	85	75	59
The church seems irrelevant to life today	20	24	48
The bible seems irrelevant to life today	23	27	53
I want my children to be baptised/christened in church	64	48	28
Christian ministers/vicars/priests do a good job	45	22	13

The issue of whether or not church attendance is a requirement of Christianity shows that atheists are much more inclined than churchgoers to see church attendance and Christianity as closely interrelated. While only 28% of atheists think it is possible to be a Christian without attending church, it is 44% of agnostics and 64% of theists who believe this; conversely, while 9% of theists and 10% of agnostics do not believe that anyone can be a Christian without attending church, it is 37% of atheists who come to this conclusion.

The reverse perspective confirms these findings except in two small respects. While 10% of atheists and 17% of theists think church is interesting, a *smaller* number of agnostics (7%) hold this view and, while 21% of atheists and 27% of theists think the bible is relevant to life today, it is the agnostics (16%) who are least likely to share this opinion.

Otherwise the figures show that 10% of theists, 14% of agnostics and 40% of atheists do not want their children baptised or christened in church; 10% of theists, 15% of agnostics and 42% of atheists think Christian ministers, vicars or priests do a bad job; 27% of theists and 16% of agnostics and atheists think the church is relevant to life today; 24% of theists, 33% of agnostics and 63% of atheists reject the idea that religious education should be taught in school; 3% of theists, 4% of agnostics and 14% of atheists would not want to marry in church and 68% of theists, 80% of agnostics and 93% of atheists reject daily religious assemblies in school.

Agnostics are most likely to be uncertain about these issues. On three matters more than half of the agnostics cannot make up their minds. As many as 63% of agnostics are uncertain if Christian ministers, vicars or priests do a good job and 60% cannot decide if the church is relevant to today's life; 57% are equally undecided about the bible. Slightly lower levels of uncertainty affect theists on two issues: 53% are unsure if the church is relevant and 50% cannot make a decision about the relevance of the bible. Even atheists, who are the least undecided group, have difficulty in assessing the sort of job the clergy are doing. As many as 45% of atheists are uncertain what to think on this matter.

Does denomination make a difference?

This section examines the responses of teenagers who attend church weekly in Roman Catholic, Anglican and Free Chur h settings to see if the denominational framework has an effect on perceptions about church and religion.

First, and overwhelmingly, there are great similarities between young Christians in these denominations. Over 90% want to get married in church (92% of Roman Catholic, 93% of Anglican and 94% of Free Church young people) and over 80% want their children to be baptised or christened in church (82% of Free Church and 88% of both Anglican and Roman Catholic young people). More than 60% approve of religious education in schools (61% of Anglican, 62% of Roman Catholic and 67% of Free Church young people).

Table 15.6   Church and Society: by denomination

	Catholic %	Anglican %	Free %
Religious education should be taught in school	62	61	67
Schools should hold a religious assembly every day	10	15	23
Church is boring	36	10	10
I believe that I can be a Christian without going to church	43	43	46
I want to get married in church	92	93	94
The church seems irrelevant to life today	18	11	15
The bible seems irrelevant to life today	21	13	13
I want my children to be baptised/christened in church	88	88	82
Christian ministers/vicars/priests do a good job	66	75	73

Second, however, there are differences in the ways these young people think about their religion. Most striking is the gap between the 36% of Roman Catholics and the 10% of both Anglican and Free Church young people on the issue of whether church is boring. Weekly churchgoing Catholics tend far more frequently to think their services are boring. The reverse perspective underlines this finding. Only 43% of Roman Catholic young people appear to find church interesting, compared with 73% of Anglican and Free Church teenagers. It is the Roman Catholics, too, who are least inclined to favour daily religious assemblies in school. Thus, while only 10% of Catholics approve of this practice, it is slightly more Anglican (15%) and Free Church (23%) young people who concur; and the reverse perspective shows that 60% of Catholics do not support daily religious assemblies, compared with 51% of Anglican and 42% of Free Church young people.

In line with these findings, Roman Catholic young people are also less confident than the others that the church or the bible are relevant to contemporary life. While only half of Roman Catholic young people (50%) think the church is relevant to life today, it is nearly two thirds (63%) of Anglican and Free Church teenagers who think this and, while less than half of Roman Catholics (44%) think the bible is relevant to life today, it is well over half of Anglican (57%) and Free Church (63%) young people who take this view. On both these matters the reverse perspective is confirmatory. Whereas 18% of Roman Catholic teenagers think the church is irrelevant to life today, it is only 15% and 11% respectively of Free Church and Anglican young people who agree with them. Whereas 21% of Roman Catholic teenagers think the bible is irrelevant to life today, it is only 13% of the other two denominational groups who share this opinion. Furthermore, fewer Roman Catholic young people give their clergy a vote of approval. Whereas 66% of Roman Catholics think their clergy are doing a good job, it is 73% of Free Church and three quarters (75%) of Anglican young people who make this assessment.

The percentages who think that it is possible to be a Christian without attending church vary very little whatever the denominational setting. As many as 27% of both Anglican and Free Church and 28% of Roman Catholic young people think that church attendance is necessary for the Christian life, but 43% of both Anglicans and Roman Catholics and 46% of Free Church young people disagree.

Implications

If pupils were given a vote on the retention or abolition of a daily religious assembly, it is clear that the stipulations with regard to collective worship in the 1988 Education Reform Act would not have been passed. Even weekly churchgoers can only muster 17% of their number in support of daily religious assemblies. The vast majority of pupils, of whatever age group or sex, do not want such gatherings. What this survey cannot answer, however, is if it is mainly the word 'daily' which sticks in the throats of these young people. Support for religious education is considerably stronger. Even 12% of atheists believe religious education ought to be taught in school and, among weekly churchgoers, the figure rises as high as 61%. Nearly two fifths of all girls (38%) approve of religious education. The study of religion in school, therefore, is acceptable to a large minority, but it is daily assemblies which pupils, in large numbers, clearly dislike. Whether the more flexible arrangements for school worship which are now possible under the 1988 Act and confirmed in Circular 1/94 will improve pupil attitudes remains to be seen.

The rites of passage offered by the church are popular and valued, even by non-churchgoers and atheists. As many as 59% of atheists would want to marry in church and, among churchgoers, the figure rises to over 90%. The same is true, to a lesser extent, of the baptism or christening of children. Over a quarter of non-churchgoing atheists (28%) would want their children baptised or christened in this way and the figure for non-churchgoers as a whole reaches two fifths (43%). Among non-churchgoing theists it rises to nearly two thirds (64%) and among weekly churchgoers it reaches 82%. There is no hostility to the church in these statistics. On the contrary, young people evidently see the role of the church as being properly associated with birth and marriage, especially marriage, and only a very small percentage (6% of boys and 4% of girls) would actually object to a church wedding. In this connection there is a general acceptance that clergy do a good job; certainly the overall number who feel competent to criticise the clergy is less than a fifth (17%). Naturally enough non-churchgoing atheists are the group most critical of the clergy (42%), but here the criticism is softened by an even larger percentage of non-churchgoing atheists (45%) who do not feel able to judge.

The main problem faced by the church is that it is seen as irrelevant by a significant minority. Oddly enough, while 27% overall see the church as irrelevant to life today, 16% of weekly and 21% of occasional churchgoers agree with this view. In other words, the opinion of many churchgoers themselves is close to the opinion of the population at large. Or, putting this another way, a significant proportion of churchgoers do not go to church primarily because they see it as being outstandingly relevant to modern life. This is not true of all churchgoers, of course, because 56% of weekly churchgoers *do* see the church as being relevant to modern life.

What the figures on the relevance of the church show most markedly is that a very large segment of the teenage population does not feel able to comment one way or the other. As many as 46% of the total population, 51% of girls, 49% of non-churchgoers, 36% of non-churchgoing atheists and 60% of non-churchgoing agnostics place themselves in the uncertain category. The reason for this uncertainty must be related to the general ignorance which young people feel themselves to have about the church; for example, as many as 27% do not know whether church is boring or not.

A similar problem affects perceptions of the bible. Roughly a quarter of the total population (27%) think the bible does have a relevance to contemporary life, and this figure is stable over both year groups and both sexes. Even a fifth (21%) of non-churchgoing atheists see the bible as a relevant book, but what the figures show most distinctly is that a huge proportion of young people feels unable to express a judgement on this matter. Overall 43% of young people do not know what to think about the bible, and this figure rises to nearly half of the girls (48%) and over half of the non-churchgoing agnostics (57%). Even a third (35%) of Roman Catholics who go to church weekly do not feel competent to pass a proper opinion. The uncertainty about the bible which mirrors uncertainty about the church suggests that many young people have not grappled with their teachings. To this extent religious education has failed to give a significant proportion of young people enough information upon which to make up their minds. This proportion probably amounts to about 20% of young people since, even on religious issues on which pupils are informed by personal experience (like daily religious assemblies), about 20% cannot decide. If we can subtract this 20% of young people who appear to have difficulty in making decisions on religious matters from the 43% who are uncertain about the bible and the 46% who are uncertain about the church, we are left with the young people whose basis for indecision is most likely to be lack of information. Moreover, 47% of young people cannot decide about the clergy, and this figure is similar to the uncertainty figures about church and bible. It is likely that at least half the young people in school have little or no contact with the clergy, and this uncertainty is therefore understandable. What is harder to understand, unless, as we have suggested, religious education has failed to convey the necessary information, is that similar numbers (between 40% and 50%) are unable to comment on the relevance of the bible and the church.

Church is perceived as being boring by more than half these teenagers, but boredom is clearly in the eye of the beholder because, whereas only 20% of weekly churchgoers see it in this light, it is 81% of non-churchgoing atheists and 61% of non-churchgoing agnostics who do so. The paradox that 65% of non-churchgoers see the church as boring may be explained by the supposition that many of them once attended or that they are responding to a generally perceived negative stereotype of the church. What is more alarming for clergy, however, is that between 10% and 36% of their churchgoing young people see church as boring. Roman Catholicism may make fewer liturgical concessions to young people, and consequently pays the price for its traditionalism in the less enthusiastic vote of its younger attenders.

Church attendance is widely regarded as being unnecessary for the Christian. Not unnaturally this view is held by occasional churchgoers, but non-churchgoing atheists also tend to have definite opinions on the matter because 37% of them take the opposite view and think it is impossible to be a Christian without church attendance. In effect many of these atheists seem to see Christianity as a matter not of belief but of observance. This may explain why over a fifth (28%) of non-churchgoing atheists want their children baptised or christened and over half (59%) want to be married in church. In effect what they are saying is, 'I am not a Christian and therefore I will not regularly attend church, but I believe the church offers a useful social ritual in which I can take part without compromising my atheistic life-style.'

The opposite explanation can be put forward to account for the difference between girls and boys over church attendance. More girls than boys think they *can* be Christians without attendance at church and fewer girls than boys think they *cannot* be Christians without attendance; in other words belief, for girls, can be more important than a public form of religious observance. Yet on the matter of church weddings the vast majority of girls (84%) show themselves to be enthusiastic. Since it is on the matter of marriage services that the church receives its most ringing endorsement by young people, we may be entitled to ask whether the future of marriage in Britain depends on the future of the church, or whether the future of the church depends on the future of marriage. But perhaps the answer to this question is that young people support the Christian rite of passage without clearly or necessarily supporting the Christian teaching on marriage.

16　Politics

Introduction
This chapter describes key political views held by young people. To gain an insight into these views ten statements were put forward. The first two refer to the two main political parties, Conservative and Labour and asserted, 'I have confidence in the Conservative/Labour party'. The third statement tested the scepticism of young people about politics as a whole and affirmed, 'It makes no difference which political party is in power'. An evaluation of local politics was sampled by the statement, 'The local council does a good job' and then there were six statements dealing with typical left or right wing policies. Two referred to race: 'There are too many black people living in this country' and 'I think that immigration into Britain should be restricted'; one referred to medicine, 'Private medicine should be abolished'; another to education, 'Private schools should be abolished'; and the last two to the work place, 'Trade Unions have too much power' and 'State ownership of industry is a good thing'.

Overview
The main national political parties attract approximately equal amounts of support, though a significant minority (19%) thinks it makes no difference which political party is in power. The figures are straightforward. While 17% of young people have confidence in the Conservative party, 19% have confidence in the Labour party. This slight preference for the Labour party is expressed by the reverse perspective since 49% of young people do not have confidence in the Conservatives and 45% do not have confidence in Labour. In the first case 34% of teenagers are uncertain and in the second 36% are uncertain. The cynicism or *laissez-faire* attitude of the 19% who do not think political parties make a difference is challenged by the 49% who

think that the political complexion of the government definitely does make a difference. When it comes to local politics, however, the local council receives the support of 18% of young people, roughly the number who support one of the two main political parties, but is criticised by 37%; 45% are uncertain.

Table 16.1   Politics: overview

	Agree %	Not certain %	Disagree %
I have confidence in the Conservative party	17	34	49
I have confidence in the Labour party	19	36	45
Private medicine should be abolished	17	42	41
It makes no difference which political party is in power	19	32	49
Private schools should be abolished	25	32	42
The local council does a good job	18	45	37
There are too many black people living in this country	19	16	65
State ownership of industry is a good thing	17	70	13
Trade Unions have too much power	24	65	11
I think that immigration into Britain should be restricted	32	38	30

Racial issues demonstrate ambivalence which we try to interpret at the end of this chapter. While 19% of young people think there are too many black people in Britain, many (32%) think that immigration should be restricted. Or, to put it another way, while 65% of young people do not think there are too many black people living in this country, only 30% think that immigration should not be restricted. Uncertainty about immigration is felt by 38% of teenagers and uncertainty about the number of black people in Britain is felt by 16%.

The abolition of private medicine is supported by 17% of young people, but 41% would retain it and 42% are unsure. Private schools attract less support: a quarter (25%) of teenagers would abolish them, but 42% would not and 32% are uncertain. Trade Union power is largely a matter of uncertainty for young people: 65% place themselves in the unsure category, but nearly a quarter (24%) agree with the general right wing position and think that Trade Unions have too much power, and only 11% take the contrary view. State ownership of industry, after more than a decade of public defence of market forces, is thought to be a good thing by less than one in five (17%) young people and only defended by just over one in eight (13%); a massive 70% are unclear about the issue.

Does gender make a difference?

There are definite gender differences in approaches to politics and political issues. In the main, girls are less racially biased and less interested in political parties than are boys. With regard to the number of black people living in Britain, the contrast between males and females is stark. Whereas 28% of boys think there are too many black people in the UK, only 11% of girls share this view, and the reverse perspective confirms this finding. While 54% of boys do not think there are too many black people in Britain, the equivalent figure for girls is over three quarters (76%). On the matter of immigration, almost twice as many boys as girls think there should be restrictions. While 22% of girls think there should be restrictions, it is 43% of boys who take this view, and the reverse perspective underlines this trend since 25% of boys think there should not be immigration restrictions, as compared with 34% of girls.

Boys are generally more inclined to support the main political parties. While 21% of boys have confidence in the Conservative party, it is only 13% of girls who agree with them; while 21% of boys have confidence in the Labour party, it is only 17% of girls who agree with them; and the reverse perspective confirms this tendency since 51% of boys do not have confidence in the Conservatives and 50% do not have confidence in Labour, as against 46% and 40% respectively of girls.

The local council receives a positive rating from 21% of boys and 15% of girls. Boys are more inclined than girls to

approve of state ownership of industry and to disapprove of
Trade Union power. While 23% of boys approve of state
ownership, it is only 11% of girls who do so; while 33% of
boys think the Trade Unions have too much power, it is
only 16% of girls who take this view. Put the other way,
17% of boys as against 9% of girls are opposed to state
ownership of industry and 13% of boys and 9% of girls
disagree that the Trade Unions have too much power.

Table 16.2   Politics: by gender

	Male %	Female %
I have confidence in the Conservative party	21	13
I have confidence in the Labour party	21	17
Private medicine should be abolished	18	15
It makes no difference which political party is in power	20	19
Private schools should be abolished	30	21
The local council does a good job	21	15
There are too many black people living in this country	28	11
State ownership of industry is a good thing	23	11
Trade Unions have too much power	33	16
I think that immigration into Britain should be restricted	43	22

The figures show that girls are very much more likely to
be uncertain about the main political parties than are boys.
While 28% of boys are uncertain about the Conservatives
and 29% uncertain about Labour, the figures for girls are
41% and 43%. Even on local politics the girls are more
likely than boys to be unsure. Whereas 37% of boys are
uncertain if the local council does a good job, the figure for
girls rises to over half (53%). Female uncertainty on
political issues spills over to the economy. An overwhelming
80% of girls are unsure what to say about state ownership
of industry and a similar number (75%) do not know if the
Trade Unions have too much power. The corresponding
figures for uncertain boys are 60% and 54%.

Private schools and private medicine show different response patterns. While 30% of boys as against 21% of girls would abolish private schools, the number of boys in favour of private schools is 41% and the number of girls is 44%. In other words there are more girls than boys in favour of private schools. When it comes to medicine, it is again more boys than girls who support abolition. While 15% of girls would abolish private medical practice, it is 18% of boys who would do so. The difference comes in the number in favour of private medicine. Here 44% of boys, as against 39% of girls, are in favour. Thus there are more boys in favour of private medicine and more boys against. We discuss these figures later in the chapter.

One item summarises characteristic differences between girls and boys as revealed in this survey. Roughly a fifth of pupils (20% of boys and 19% of girls) think that it makes no difference which political party is in power. This group is the sceptical minority. A large middle group is uncertain about the matter, with more girls than boys uncertain (26% of boys and 38% of girls). The third group, just over half of boys (54%) and just over two out of five girls (43%), thinks that it does make a difference which party is in power. This is the group which shows signs of political awareness.

Does age make a difference?

The development of political opinion reveals an interesting pattern. With two main exceptions political opinions remain largely static between years nine and ten.

It is the issue of race which provides the first exception. Whereas the numbers of those who agree with the statements on the Conservative party, the Labour party, private medicine, which political party is in power and the Trade Unions show no alteration at all as pupils get older, there is a shift of 7% in the number of pupils in favour of immigration restrictions. While 29% of year nine pupils think there should be restrictions, the figure rises to 36% by year ten, and the reverse perspective confirms the trend. There are slightly more pupils who think there should be no immigration restrictions in the younger age group, 30% in year nine and 29% in year ten. The reduction in uncertainty on this item (41% of pupils in year nine and 35% of pupils in year ten) speaks of a hardening of attitudes. As further evidence of this shift the item dealing with the number of black people living in this country records a similar change. Just under a fifth (18%) of pupils in year nine think there are too many black people living in Britain, and this figure rises to just over a fifth (21%) in year ten; simultaneously the percentage of pupils who do not think there are too many black people falls from 67% in year nine to 63% in year ten.

Table 16.3   Politics: by age

	Year 9 %	Year 10 %
I have confidence in the Conservative party	17	17
I have confidence in the Labour party	19	19
Private medicine should be abolished	16	16
It makes no difference which political party is in power	19	19
Private schools should be abolished	26	24
The local council does a good job	19	17
There are too many black people living in this country	18	21
State ownership of industry is a good thing	16	18
Trade Unions have too much power	24	24
I think that immigration into Britain should be restricted	29	36

The second exception is provided by the local council. Disaffection increases. In year nine 19% of pupils think the council does a good job, but only 17% of pupils in year ten make this positive assessment. The reverse perspective confirms this opinion because the 35% of pupils in year nine who think the local council does not do a good job turns to 38% in year ten.

An interesting development of political opinion is shown on many items by the reverse perspective. Thus, while there is no change between years nine and ten in the 16% of pupils who think that private medicine should be abolished, there *is* a difference in those who think that private medicine should not be abolished, from 40% in year nine to 44% in year ten. Likewise, while 24% of pupils in years nine and ten think that Trade Unions have too much power, there is a shift from 10% to 13% in the same time span between those who think the Trade Unions do not have too much power; or, while 19% of pupils in both years nine and ten think that it does not make a difference which political party is in power, 48% of year nine pupils and 50% of year ten pupils disagree with this sceptical viewpoint. Similarly, there is a larger shift in years nine and ten (41% and 45% respectively) between those who do not think private schools should be abolished, than between those who do (26% in year nine and 24% in year ten).

Into this set of figures we should note that, while 16% of year nine pupils think that state ownership of industry is a good thing, a higher number (18%) of year ten pupils take this view; yet a contrary trend is demonstrated by the 12% of pupils in year nine who do not think state ownership is a good thing and the higher number (14%) who agree with them in year ten.

Finally, there is a consistent trend for the uncertainty figures to drop by a few percent between years nine and ten. The largest drops concern immigration (from 41% to 35%), state ownership of industry (72% to 68%) and private medicine (44% to 40%). We discuss the significance of all these findings at the end of this chapter.

Does church attendance make a difference?

This section examines pupils' attitudes towards politics in the light of their church attendance and makes comparison between three groups: those who never attend church, those who attend church sometimes and those who attend church nearly every week.

The sharpest difference between weekly churchgoers and non-churchgoers concerns racial issues. Churchgoers are much more inclined to accept immigration and black people than are non-churchgoers. While 11% of weekly churchgoers think there are too many black people in Britain, the figure for occasional churchgoers is 16% and for non-churchgoers is 24%; in the reverse perspective the same trend shows because, while 60% of non-churchgoers do not think there are too many black people in Britain, the comparable figure for occasional churchgoers is 69% and for weekly church-goers is 77%. Restrictions on immigration are supported by over a quarter of weekly churchgoers (27%) and by over a third of non-churchgoers (34%), and the occasional church-goers fall in the middle at 32%; in the same way the percentage of weekly churchgoers against immigration restrictions is 36%, but a lower number of non-churchgoers (27%) and an intermediate number of occasional church-goers (30%) hold this position.

Table 16.4   Politics: by church attendance

	Weekly %	Sometimes %	Never %
I have confidence in the Conservative party	17	19	16
I have confidence in the Labour party	19	19	20
Private medicine should be abolished	14	15	18
It makes no difference which political party is in power	17	18	21
Private schools should be abolished	20	23	28
The local council does a good job	21	18	17
There are too many black people living in this country	11	16	24
State ownership of industry is a good thing	16	17	17
Trade Unions have too much power	22	23	25
I think that immigration into Britain should be restricted	27	32	34

The two main political parties attract approximately equal support from weekly and occasional churchgoers, but a slightly higher number of non-churchgoers favours Labour. Among weekly churchgoers 17% have confidence in the Conservatives and 19% have confidence in Labour. Con-versely 47% of weekly churchgoers do not rely on the

Conservative party and 43% have no confidence in Labour. If anything, weekly churchgoers are more inclined to Labour than to the Conservatives. Just over half (51%) of non-churchgoers have no confidence in the Conservative party and 46% lack confidence in Labour. Speaking positively, 16% of non-churchgoers trust the Conservatives and slightly more (20%) trust Labour. Occasional attenders fall in the middle of these figures (19% support Conservative, 19% support Labour, 45% do not trust the Conservatives and 44% do not trust Labour).

The political leanings of churchgoers and non-church-goers are revealed by their stances on private medicine and schools. But this stance, as we shall see, must not be taken simplistically. For, while more weekly churchgoers than other groups support private medicine and private schools, fewer weekly churchgoers think the Trade Unions have too much power. The figures are as follows: 14% of weekly churchgoers would abolish private medicine, as against 15% of occasional churchgoers and 18% of non-churchgoers, and this finding is confirmed by the reverse perspective where 42% of weekly churchgoers, as against 41% of both occasional and non-churchgoers, would retain private medicine. In the same way, 20% of weekly churchgoers would abolish private schools, as compared with 23% of occasional churchgoers and 28% of non-churchgoers; conversely, 48% of weekly churchgoers would retain private schools, against a lower number of occasional churchgoers (45%) and an even lower number of non-churchgoers (39%). While 22% of weekly churchgoers and 23% of occasional churchgoers think the Trade Unions have too much power, the figure for non-churchgoers is 25%. The reverse perspective on this item shows a close set of figures not quite matching the statistics on agreement: while 10% of weekly churchgoers do not think the Trade Unions have too much power, it is 11% of non-churchgoers and 12% of occasional churchgoers who take this view.

Churchgoers have a stronger disposition to approve of their local councils. While 21% of weekly churchgoers think their council does a good job, it is 17% of non-churchgoers who take this view; from the position of those who disapprove of their council, the gap between weekly churchgoers (30%) and non-churchgoers (40%) is significant.

Churchgoers also have a slightly greater sense of the value of political activity. While 17% of weekly churchgoers and 18% of occasional churchgoers think it makes no difference which party is in power, the corresponding figure for non-churchgoers is 21%. Viewed the other way, half (50%) of weekly and occasional churchgoers think it makes a difference which party is in power, whereas only 47% of non-churchgoers take this view.

Teenagers are not sure about major economic issues. The vast majority are uncertain about state ownership of industry and they obviously do not learn much on this subject in church. While 69% of non-churchgoers are unclear on the matter, the figure for occasional churchgoers is 71% and for weekly churchgoers 72%. However, overall there is a slight bias in favour of state ownership because 16% of weekly churchgoers and 17% of occasional churchgoers and non-churchgoers support this form of economic management, compared with 12% of both weekly and occasional churchgoers and 14% of non-churchgoers who do not.

Does belief in God make a difference?

We now look in detail at those who do not attend a church and explore the difference in the opinions of three distinct groups: 'theists', 'agnostics' and 'atheists' (see page 7).

Non-churchgoing theists turn out to be more inclined to have confidence in Labour (25%) than the Conservatives (19%), a finding supported by the percentages who lack confidence in these two parties. Whereas 49% of theists do not have confidence in the Conservatives, it is only 41% of theists who are unconfident about Labour.

Agnostics about God are also inclined to be agnostic about politics and economics. The highest number of uncertain responses to the statements on the Conservative and Labour parties and on state ownership of industry come from the agnostics. While 39% of agnostics are uncertain about the Conservatives and 41% about Labour, the comparable figures for theists are 32% and 34% and for atheists 28% in both cases. Otherwise the agnostics are also slightly more likely to favour the Labour party. While 46% of agnostics do not have confidence in the Conservatives, only 41% do not have confidence in Labour; conversely 15% trust the Conservatives and 18% trust Labour. Three quarters (75%) of agnostics are uncertain about state ownership of industry, compared with 71% of theists and 63% of atheists.

Table 16.5   Politics: by belief among non-churchgoers

	Theist %	Agnostic %	Atheist %
I have confidence in the Conservative party	19	15	15
I have confidence in the Labour party	25	18	18
Private medicine should be abolished	20	15	19
It makes no difference which political party is in power	19	19	23
Private schools should be abolished	25	26	31
The local council does a good job	22	16	15
There are too many black people living in this country	20	20	29
State ownership of industry is a good thing	18	15	19
Trade Unions have too much power	23	22	29
I think that immigration into Britain should be restricted	31	30	38

Atheists show themselves more likely than the other two groups to be against both the main political parties and the local council. The figures are clear. Over half of atheists do not have confidence in the Conservatives (57%) and a similar number does not trust the Labour party either (54%). Put the other way, less than a fifth (18%) of atheists have confidence in Labour and only 15% trust the Conservatives. Fewer atheists (15%) than agnostics (16%) or theists (22%) think the local council does a good job, and this finding is confirmed by the percentages of those critical of the local council. While 34% of agnostics and 35% of theists are critical of their council, the figure for atheists is noticeably higher at 48%.

There is also a tendency for some atheists to lack confidence in the political process as a whole. A larger number of atheists (23%) thinks it makes no difference which political party is in power than is the case for theists and agnostics (19%). But this finding is not clear-cut because the same percentage of theists and atheists (49%) think that it *does* make a difference which party is in power.

Private medicine and schools again show that they are distinct issues to which teenagers apply different principles. While 15% of agnostics would abolish private medicine, it is 19% of atheists and 20% of theists who would do so. Yet the greatest support for private medicine comes from atheists. Nearly half (47%) of atheists would retain private medicine, compared with 37% of agnostics and 38% of theists. Private schools, however, would be abolished by 31% of atheists, 26% of agnostics and 25% of theists. They would be retained by only 37% of agnostics, 40% of atheists and 43% of theists.

Atheists show a tendency, compared with the other two groups, to take a negative view of black people. While 20% of both theists and agnostics think there are too many black people in Britain, the figure for atheists rises to 29%. The solidity of this finding is confirmed by the reverse perspective. While 56% of atheists do not think there are too many black people in Britain, it is 62% of agnostics and 64% of theists who take this view. Likewise, there is a tendency for atheists to be more inclined than the other groups to support immigration restrictions. Just under a third of agnostics (30%) and theists (31%) support immigration restrictions as against 38% of atheists. The reverse perspective shows that this tendency is differentiated because, while slightly more theists (29%) than atheists (28%) oppose immigration restrictions, there are fewer agnostics (27%) who take the same position.

Atheists are both more inclined to support and more inclined to be critical of Trade Union power and state ownership of industry than are the other two groups. While 22% of agnostics and 23% of theists think the Trade Unions have too much power, it is 29% of atheists who take this view. On the other hand the 9% of agnostics and 11% of theists who think the Trade Unions do not have too much power are outnumbered by the 14% of atheists who take this view. While 15% of agnostics and 18% of theists agree that state ownership of industry is a good thing, it is 19% of atheists who take a similar position. On the other hand, while 10% of agnostics and 11% of theists disagree with state ownership, it is a significantly higher 18% of atheists who agree with them. We discuss the pattern of political responses by atheists at the end of this chapter.

Does denomination make a difference?

The previous section looked at those who never attend church. This section examines those who attend weekly, either in an Anglican, Free Church or Roman Catholic setting.

Table 16.6　Politics: by denomination

	Catholic %	Anglican %	Free %
I have confidence in the Conservative party	17	20	13
I have confidence in the Labour party	23	16	18
Private medicine should be abolished	14	13	11
It makes no difference which political party is in power	17	17	14
Private schools should be abolished	22	15	21
The local council does a good job	17	23	21
There are too many black people living in this country	10	10	8
State ownership of industry is a good thing	16	18	16
Trade Unions have too much power	25	20	20
I think that immigration into Britain should be restricted	29	25	25
	10	10	8

The differences between the denominations are noticeable in two main areas. First, there is a tendency for more Anglicans to have confidence in the Conservative party than do the other two groups. This is shown both by the positive and negative figures. More Anglican than Roman Catholic or Free Church teenagers have confidence in the Conservatives and fewer lack confidence in them. The figures are: 13% of Free Church teenagers, 17% of Roman Catholics and 20% of Anglicans have confidence in the Conservatives; 52% of the Roman Catholics, 49% of the Free Church teenagers and only 41% of the Anglicans lack confidence in the Conservatives.

Support for Labour tends to belong to the other church groups. While 16% of Anglicans have confidence in Labour, it is 18% of Free Church teenagers and 23% of Roman Catholics who share this trust; conversely, while 39% of Free Church teenagers and 40% of Roman Catholics do not trust Labour, the figure for Anglicans is rather more (46%).

It would be a mistake to read the slight preference for Labour among Roman Catholics superficially. There are actually more Roman Catholics (25%) who think the Trade Unions have too much power than is the case with either Anglican (20%) or Free Church (20%) teenagers. There are also more Roman Catholics (17%) than Anglicans (10%) and Free Church (8%) teenagers who disagree with state ownership of industry.

Whatever support there is for the two main political parties among teenage churchgoers needs to be read alongside support for the political process as a whole. The differences between the three denominational groupings are ambiguous. While 17% of Anglican and Roman Catholic young people think it makes no difference which political party is in power, fewer Free Church young people (14%) share this view; yet, fewer Free Church young people (48%) than Anglicans (51%) and Roman Catholics (52%) think it does make a difference which party occupies Downing Street or City Hall. Putting this another way, only about half of churchgoing young people think that political choices make a difference to their lives.

Second, there is a tendency for Anglicans to support private schools. Over half of Anglicans (55%) would retain private schools, compared with 45% of Roman Catholic and 42% of Free Church young people. This finding, however, should not be seen as a great vote of confidence in private schools among Anglicans since 21% of them would favour abolition. The comparable figure for Roman Catholics is 22% and for Free Church young people is 15%.

All the other figures show less than 5% variation, and most less than 3%.

Implications

These figures show that political opinions form later in life than religious opinions. The percentages of pupils who have confidence in a particular political party are about half the percentages who believe in God or believe that Jesus is the Son of God. And, to the extent that political and economic opinions are connected, the very large measure of uncertainty among teenagers on state ownership of industry or Trade Union power adds to this impression. It would be true, but misleading, to say that British pupils have more confidence in God than they do in either of the two main political parties. It would be true because the figures show it to be true, but it would be misleading because the belief which young people have in God is likely to be psychologically different from the confidence which they have in political parties. British teenagers are certainly not highly political. In fact evaluation of the local council, with which the majority will have more direct contact than they do with the main political parties, attracts a large measure of uncertainty (45%).

Whatever the general political indifference or ignorance of most British teenagers, they show strong feelings on racial issues. Of all the statements presented to teenagers in this chapter, the one which attracted the lowest level of uncertainty concerned the number of black people in Britain. Altogether nearly a fifth of young people think there are too many black people in Britain. It is from this limited segment of teenagers that racist groups have recruited or will recruit support. Yet, racist views are clearly in the minority. There are more than three times as many young people who do not think there are too many black people in Britain.

The figures concerning restriction on immigration may have a racist or an economic thrust, but the evidence could be interpreted to suggest that they do stem from a racist motivation since the groups which support immigration restriction (boys rather than girls, year ten pupils rather than year nine pupils, non-churchgoing atheists rather than non-churchgoing theists) are also more likely to agree with the statement, 'There are too many black people living in this country'.

Whatever signs of prejudice the figures point to, however, it is also clear that British teenagers cannot be said to be mainly racist in orientation. On the two relevant items, the only matter on which more than half of teenagers agree (65%) is that there are *not* too many black people in Britain.

The figures on private schools and private medicine suggest that young people are in favour of choice. More than twice as many young people would retain private medicine and private schools as support either of the two main political parties.

The pattern of figures on private medicine shows that there are more boys than girls in favour of it and more boys than girls against it. The same sort of pattern can be seen among non-churchgoing atheists over the power of Trade Unions and state ownership of industry. This suggests that there are subgroups among boys and subgroups among non-churchgoing atheists. This is especially likely as neither of the two issues affects the defining characteristic of the group: atheism and Trade Unionism are definitionally independent and private medicine is unconnected with gender. We could speculate that what is happening in these instances is that fewer boys and non-churchgoing atheists are prepared to say they are not sure. In other words, boys and atheists are unwilling to live with uncertainty and therefore opt for one end of the scale or the other. Further research is needed to clarify the issue.

The age trend suggests a gradually developing political consciousness. The issues on which pupils make up their minds between years nine and ten tend to be those which affect them directly or indirectly: schooling, the economy (and therefore job prospects), the local council and other ethnic groups (with whom there may be competition for jobs). Certainly there is a fall in uncertainty on economic matters within the year as many pupils begin to think of exams and leaving school.

Churchgoers, of whichever denominational group, demonstrate far fewer racist attitudes than non-churchgoers. Whatever else may be said about the church, it is apparent that it is an international and multi-racial community or collection of communities with social opinions, in many respects, quite separate from those of the surrounding society.

Conclusion

During the course of analysing the data generated by this survey we have been struck by four sets of practical recommendations which arise from it. These are addressed to clergy, teachers, adult educators and parents.

Clergy need to take account of the prevalence of suicidal thoughts among young people, to understand the latent activism of young people, to appreciate the likely sexual backgrounds of young people coming forward for church marriages and to take pastoral steps to help Christian young people to cope with the sexual expectations of the vast majority of mid-teenagers. Roman Catholic clergy need to be aware that Roman Catholic teaching on abortion is far more widely accepted among the young than its teaching on birth control. The tension for both young people and clergy needs a proper resolution.

Teachers need to be aware of the fear of bullying, especially among girls, which affects a surprising number of 13 to 15 year olds and to do their best to remove its causes. There is also a case for renewing the anti-smoking drive whose effectiveness looks as if it is waning. Girls, more than boys, are prone to be attracted to cigarettes. The painful inability of some young people to form relationships with the opposite sex is, no doubt, all part of 'growing up', but it is a matter to which teachers could usefully give attention, especially if they are to be seen as more approachable by young people. Finally, religious education has, for many young people, failed to give them the basic information needed on which to make a judgement about either the church or the bible.

Adult educators need to take action to help young people with parenting skills. The figures show how difficult it is for some teenagers to talk to their fathers. The stress which is placed upon the mother in these situations needs to be faced and eased. Though this survey has been about young people and their values, it would appear that it is still the mother who for most young people is the crucial figure in their lives.

Parents who have good relationships with their children may intuitively have appreciated some of the problems uncovered by this research, yet the incidence of a feeling of depression (53%), for example, and the concerns which many young people have for the environment (66%) may come as a matter of surprise. Certainly, in the teenage years it is important for parents to be available to their children and to be able to offer advice without condemnation and support without inhibiting the growth of teenage autonomy. The finding that 56% of girls and 36% of boys find it unhelpful to talk with their fathers suggests that there is enormous room for improvement. Ideally, surely, parents should be able to identify the concerns and worries of their teenage children and help to share the former and reduce the latter. Only if parents consciously adopt such aims and give them a high priority are they likely to attain success.

Index